ICSE

POEMS WORKBOOK

(For Class X)

ICSE Examination Year 2025 onwards

Wallace Jacob

INDIA • SINGAPORE • MALAYSIA

ISBN 979-8-89556-329-8

Contents

Preface

In his seminal article *What is a Poem?*, Eliseo Vivas (1954) explains that a poem is a linguistic artifact, whose function is to organize the primary data of experience that can be exhibited in and through words and poetry uniquely reveals a world which is self-sufficient.

Several savants such as C. L. Stevenson (1957), W. H. Poteat (1957), A. R. Kelkar (1969), J. Thome (1989), B. Bourbon (2007) have defined 'Poem'.

I feel that a poem conveys a deep message through words which might or might not be rhyming. A poem might be based on a person, event, object, place, circumstance, nature or emotion. In one way, poems force the reader to think. Poems might also help the reader in gaining an understanding of the world and sometimes provide deep insights into life. Some of the poets dissect the different facets of human life with great clinical acuity. Some poets dwell on difficult questions, some on historical events, some on pain and suffering, some on politics and some on social struggles.

Poems can be used for explaining the concepts of "deep structure", "surface structure", and "glossematics". This workbook is my humble endeavor to understand a few poems and to present those understandings. I modestly accept that my understanding is highly limited. I earnestly solicit criticism of this workbook (wallace_jacob@yahoo.co.in).

This workbook contains cues to a few questions. The reader is advised to verify the veracity of the cues on his/her own.

Some words in the English Language might have more than one meaning. The meaning(s) of the words in this workbook are based on the context in which the words are used in the text. I referred to *Webster's Encyclopedic Unabridged Dictionary of the English Language New Revised Edition* for the meanings which appear herein.

I thank the Almighty for this workbook and I acknowledge that left to my own I will not be able to even lift a pencil or a pen.

Wallace Jacob

Acknowledgements

I am thankful to my maternal grandparents, paternal grandparents, Mr. Vishwanath Mishra and family, Mr Sadarat Khaldy and family.

– Wallace Jacob

A Note to ICSE Students

While trying to analyze a poem the reader should focus on the
form of the poem,
language of the poem,
meaning(s) of the words used in the poem,
message(s) which the poem conveys, and
sound of the poem.

Poems might be of different types. A few types are:
ballad
blank verse
ekphrastic
elegy
epic
free verse
lyric poetry
narrative
ode
pastoral poetry
prose poetry
satire
sonnet (poem of fourteen lines)
villanelle (poem of nineteen lines).

A *ballad* is a simple, often crude, narrative poem of popular origin, composed in short stanzas, especially one of romantic character and adapted for singing.

Blank verse is unrhymed verse, especially the unrhymed iambic pentameter most frequently used in English dramatic epic, and reflective verse.

An *ekphrastic poem* is a literary description of or commentary on a visual work of art.

An *elegy* is a mournful, melancholy, or plaintive poem, especially a funeral song or a lament for the dead.

An *epic* is a poetic composition, usually centered upon a hero, in which a series of great achievements or events is narrated continuously and at length in elevated style.

A *free verse* does not follow a fixed metrical pattern.

A *lyric* has the form and musical quality of a song, and especially the character of a songlike outpouring of the poet's own thoughts and feelings.

A *narrative* is a story of events, experiences, or the like, whether true or fictitious.

An *ode* is a lyric poem typically of elaborate or irregular metrical form and expressive of exalted or enthusiastic emotion. An *ode* is a poem intended to be sung.

Pastoral poetry deals with the life of shepherds, commonly in a conventional or artificial manner, or with simple rural life.

Prose is the ordinary form of spoken or written language, without metrical structure.

Satire is a literary composition, in verse or prose, in which human folly and vice are held up to scorn, derision, or ridicule.

A *sonnet* is a poem properly expressive of a single, complete thought, idea, or sentiment, of 14 lines, usually in iambic pentameter, with rhymes arranged according to one of certain definite schemes, being in the strict or Italian form divided into a major group of 8 lines (the octave) followed by a minor group of six lines (the sestet), and in a common English form into 3 quatrains followed by a couplet.

A *villanelle* is a short poem of fixed form, written in tercets, usually five in number, followed by a final quatrain, all being based on two rhymes.

POETRY

(Treasure Chest – A Collection of ICSE Poems and Short Stories)

Poems in syllabus (according to https://cisce.org/wp-content/uploads/2024/01/1.-ICSE-English_25.pdf retrieved on 02 June 2025 at 1838 hours):

- Haunted Houses – *H. W. Longfellow*
- The Glove and the Lions – *Leigh Hunt*
- When Great Trees Fall – *Maya Angelou*
- A Considerable Speck – *Robert Frost*
- The Power of Music – *Sukumar Ray*

Haunted Houses

– Henry Wadsworth Longfellow

All houses wherein men have lived and died
Are haunted houses. Through the open doors
The harmless phantoms on their errands glide,
With feet that make no sound upon the floors.

We meet them at the door way, on the stair,
Along the passages they come and go,
Impalpable impressions on the air,
A sense of something moving to and fro.

There are more guests at table than the hosts
Invited; the illuminated hall
Is thronged with quiet, inoffensive ghosts,
As silent as the pictures on the wall.

The stranger at my fireside cannot see
The forms I see, nor hear the sounds I hear;
He but perceives what is; while unto me
All that has been is visible and clear.

We have no title-deeds to house or lands;
Owners and occupants of earlier dates
From graves forgotten stretch their dusty hands,
And hold in mortmain still their old estates.

> The author of this workbook retrieved the poem *Haunted Houses* from: https://poets.org/poem/haunted-houses (02 June 2024, 1913 hours)

> The poem *Haunted Houses* was published in 1858.

The spirit-world around this world of sense
Floats like an atmosphere, and everywhere
Wafts through these earthly mists and vapoursdense
A vital breath of more ethereal air.

Our little lives are kept in equipoise
By opposite attractions and desires;
The struggle of the instinct that enjoys,
And the more noble instinct that aspires.

These perturbations, this perpetual jar
Of earthly wants and aspirations high,
Come from the influence of an unseen star,
An undiscovered planet in our sky.

And as the moon from some dark gate of cloud
Throws o'er the sea a floating bridge of light,
Across whose trembling planks our fancies crowd
Into the realm of mystery and night,–

So from the world of spirits there descends
A bridge of light, connecting it with this,
O'er whose unsteady floor, that sways and bends,
Wander our thoughts above the dark abyss.

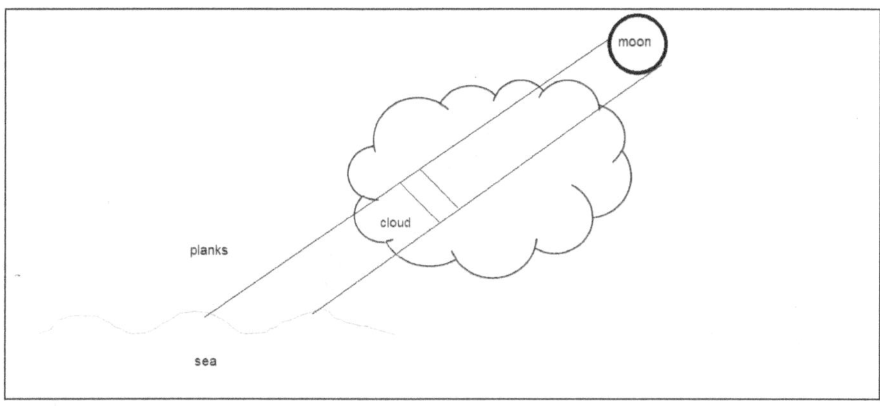

Figure 1. The terms/words '*moon*', '*dark gate of cloud*', '*bridge of light*', '*sea*', '*planks*' appear in the ninth stanza of the poem *Haunted Houses.*

Word		**Meaning**
Haunted	:	inhabited or frequented by ghosts
House	:	a building in which people live
Home	:	a house, apartment, or other shelter that is the usual residence of a person, family, or household
wherein	:	in what or in which
phantom	:	an apparition or specter
glide	:	to move smoothly and continuously along, as if without effort or resistance
Impalpable	:	incapable of being perceived by the sense of touch
perceive	:	to become aware of, know, or identify by means of the senses
title-deed	:	a deed or document containing or constituting evidence of ownership

mortmain	:	the condition of lands or tenements held without right of alienation, as by an ecclesiastical corporation; inalienable ownership, the perpetual holding of land, especially by a corporation or charitable trust
estate	:	a piece of landed property, especially one of large extent with an elaborate house on it
Waft	:	to carry lightly and smoothly through the air or over water
mist	:	a cloudlike aggregation of minute globules of water suspended in the atmosphere at or near the earth's surface
vital	:	of or pertaining to life
ethereal	:	light, airy
equipoise	:	equilibrium
perturbation	:	mental disquiet or agitation
perpetual	:	continuing or enduring forever
jar	:	a broad-mouthed container, usually cylindrical and of glass or earthenware
bridge	:	a structure spanning and affording passage over a river, chasm, road, or the like
plank	:	a long, flat piece of timber, thicker than a board
fancy	:	the artistic ability of creating unreal or whimsical imagery
realm	:	the region, sphere, or domain within which anything occurs, prevails, or dominates

descend	:	to slope, tend, or lead downward
abyss	:	a deep, immeasurable space

Punctuation marks statistics

Number of apostrophes: 02
Number of commas: 20
Number of semi-colons: 05
Number of full-stops (period symbols): 10
Number of dashes: 01
Number of hyphens: 02

Longfellow's *Haunted Houses* majestically uses the natural world around us and transforms a mundane place into a portal where he meets the supernatural. Longfellow portrays the ghosts more as acquaintances rather than as the stereotypical wisps of horror. The phantoms in *Haunted Houses* are not poltergeists (poltergeist: a ghost or spirit supposed to manifest its presence by noises, knockings, etc.). They are not angry and do not wish to take revenge.

In a way, the poem delivers a message that we (human beings) should be observant, we should be good listeners. Sometimes, knowledge might be hidden, but if we earnestly attempt to gain knowledge then some unseen forces might lead us to hidden knowledge. There might be bridges which can lead us from ignorance to knowledge, but we need have a desire for gaining knowledge and we need to translate that desire into action(s). The poem enables the reader to comprehend that there can be several unknown truths beneath our illusory connection with this world.

Henry Wadsworth Longfellow (27 Feb 1807 – 1882)

H. W. Longfellow was born to Zilpah Wadsworth and Stephen Longfellow. Longfellow was born in Portland, Maine, and attended Bowdoin College.

Longfellow studied in Germany, France, Spain and Italy. Longfellow had also taken up a teaching position at Harvard.

Major works:
Voices of the Night (1839)
Ballads and Other Poems (1842)
The Seaside and the Fireside (1850)
Evangeline: A Tale of Acadie (1847)
The Song of Hiawatha (1855)
Tales of a Wayside Inn (1863)

Read the following extracts from H. W. Longfellow's poem, '*Haunted Houses*' and answer the questions that follow:

Question 1.

All houses wherein men have lived and died
Are haunted houses. Through the open doors
The harmless phantoms on their errands glide,
With feet that make no sound upon the floors.

(i) Explain: "*harmless phantoms*".

____

____

____

(ii) Where, according to the poet, can we meet the harmless phantoms?

We meet the harmless phantoms at the door way, on the stair, along the passages as impalpable impressions on the air, at the table, in the illuminated hall.

(iii) According to the poet who (the guests or the hosts) are more in number?

According to the poet there are more guests at table than the hosts.

(iv) In his poem the poet mentions a stranger at his fireside. How is the stranger at the poet's fireside different from the poet?

The stranger at the fireside cannot see the forms which the poet-narrator is able to see. He cannot hear the sounds that the poet-narrator can hear. He can only perceive things that exist physically, while to the poet-narrator all that has been is visible and clear.

(v) What does the poet say about '*The spirit-world around this world of sense*'?

The spirit-world around this world of sense

Floats like an atmosphere, and everywhere

Wafts through these earthly mists and vapoursdense

A vital breath of more ethereal air.

(vi) What does the poet say about '*Our little lives*'?

Our little lives are kept in equipoise

By opposite attractions and desires;

The struggle of the instinct that enjoys,

And the more noble instinct that aspires.

Question 2.

We meet them at the door way, on the stair,
Along the passages they come and go,
Impalpable impressions on the air,
A sense of something moving to and fro.

[The stanza portrays the ghosts as nonchalantly walking around in the house as if it were their own home and not causing any trouble to the living beings in the house.]

(i) Whom does '*them*' in "*We meet them at the door way, on the stair*" refer to?

In "*We meet them at the door way, on the stair*", "*them*" refers to the harmless phantoms.

(ii) According to the poet which houses are '*haunted houses*'?

According to the poet all houses wherein men have lived and died are haunted houses.

(iii) To which type of place is the reader invited to in the poem?

The ditty welcomes the reader to a place where

"*The spirit-world around this world of sense*

Floats like an atmosphere, and everywhere

Wafts through these earthly mists and vapoursdense

A vital breath of more ethereal air."

(iv) Give an example of alliteration, allusion, imagery, metaphor, simile, onomatopoeia, repetition, personification in Longfellow's poem '*Haunted Houses*'.

alliteration: the commencement of two or more stressed syllables of a word group either with the same consonant sound or sound group; the commencement of two or more words of a word group with the same letter.

allusion: a passing or casual reference; an incidental mention of something, either directly or by implication.

imagery: figurative description or illustration; rhetorical images collectively.

metaphor: the application of a word or phrase to an object or concept which it does not literally denote, in order to suggest comparison with another object or concept.

simile: a figure of speech in which two unlike things are explicitly compared.

onomatopoeia: the formation of a word by imitation of a sound made by or associated with its referent.

repetition: reiteration.

personification: the attribution of personal nature or character to inanimate objects or abstract notions, especially as a rhetorical figure.

____

____

____

(v) List the terms from the poem which paint the spirits as friendly or as spirits which do not wish to harm human beings.

"*harmless phantoms*"

"*Impalpable impressions on the air*"

"*quiet, inoffensive ghosts,*
As silent as the pictures on the wall"

"*The spirit-world around this world of sense*
Floats like an atmosphere, and everywhere
Wafts through these earthly mists and vapoursdense
A vital breath of more ethereal air"

(vi) How are the ghosts portrayed in the ditty?

____

____

____

Question 3.

We have no title-deeds to house or lands;
Owners and occupants of earlier dates
From graves forgotten stretch their dusty hands,
And hold in mortmain still their old estates.

[The (fifth) stanza explains that we actually do not own the places we live in. Our ancestors or the people who lived before us in the place we live in, are the actual owners.]

(i) What is a title-deed?

____

____

____

(ii) Explain: mortmain. What is an estate?

____

____

____

(iii) How does the poet link the physical world with the spirit-world?

The spirit-world around this world of sense
Floats like an atmosphere, and everywhere
Wafts through these earthly mists and vapoursdense
A vital breath of more ethereal air.

So from the world of spirits there descends
A bridge of light, connecting it with this,

O'er whose unsteady floor, that sways and bends,

Wander our thoughts above the dark abyss.

(iv) What does the poet say about "*Our little lives*"?

Our little lives are kept in equipoise

By opposite attractions and desires;

The struggle of the instinct that enjoys,

And the more noble instinct that aspires.

(v) What message does the poem "*Haunted Houses*" convey?

____

____

____

Question 4.

The spirit-world around this world of sense
Floats like an atmosphere, and everywhere
Wafts through these earthly mists and vapoursdense
A vital breath of more ethereal air.

(i) List any *five* senses.

Our senses help us in navigating the world.

The five basic human senses are: hearing, sight, smell, taste (bitter, salty, sour, sweet) and touch (pressure, vibration).

The sense organs are ears, eyes, nose, tongue and nerve cells in the skin. The sense organs/neurons transmit the information to the brain.

Muscular sense (proprioception), sense of balance (equilibrioception), pruriception (itch), nociception (dangerous temperatures, dangerous chemicals, mechanical damage), thermoception (coolness, warmth), vomeronasal, interoception (heart beat, blood pressure, blood carbon dioxide, blood oxygen, lung stretch, cerebrospinal fluid pH) are also types of senses.

There are several disorders such as: vestibular nerve disorders, labyrinth disorders, smell disorders (anosmia, dysosmia, hyposmia) which can affect some of the senses.

(ii) What is atmosphere?

An atmosphere is made of the layers of gases surrounding a planet (or other celestial body). The atmosphere of the Earth comprises 78% nitrogen, 21% oxygen and 1% other gases.

The atmosphere of the earth can be segmented into: homosphere and heterosphere.

The atmosphere can also be divided into: troposphere, stratosphere, mesosphere, thermosphere, magnetosphere, exosphere.

(iii) Give the meanings of the following words in the context of the stanza:

Wafts, mists, vapoursdense, vital, ethereal

Wafts: floats, carried through the air

mists: cloudlike aggregation of minute globules of water suspended in the atmosphere at or near the earth's surface

vapours: gaseous particles; dense: having the component parts closely compacted together

vital: essential

ethereal: refined

___

___

___

(iv) Explain the meaning of:

The spirit-world around this world of sense
Floats like an atmosphere, and everywhere
Wafts through these earthly mists and vapoursdense
A vital breath of more ethereal air.

The world of spirits flows around us, i.e., the plane where spirits reside and the plane where human beings reside are seamlessly connected with each other. Air is essential for human beings. The world of spirits floats like an atmosphere around us and through the mists and dense vapours wafts more refined air.

[The *spirit-world* refers to the world of spirits. The *world of sense* refers to the physical world in which human-beings reside. The words *mists* and *vapoursdense* indicate barriers which are permeable. The spirit-world permeates through the earthly mists and vapoursdense into the physical-world. The spirit-world is more refined and it breathes vitality into the physical world.]

(v) What does the poet say pertaining to owners and occupants of earlier dates in the poem *Haunted Houses*?

Owners and occupants of earlier dates
From graves forgotten stretch their dusty hands,
And hold in mortmain still their old estates.

(vi) How does Longfellow describe the human condition in the poem?

Our little lives are kept in equipoise
By opposite attractions and desires;
The struggle of the instinct that enjoys,
And the more noble instinct that aspires.

Question 5.

Our little lives are kept in equipoise
By opposite attractions and desires;
The struggle of the instinct that enjoys,
And the more noble instinct that aspires.

[There are four fundamental forces that explain most of the interactions in nature: gravity, weak nuclear interaction, electromagnetic force, strong nuclear force.

Ruin might teach us to ruminate. Rumination might provide illumination which might help us discover pathways to success.]

(i) Explain the meaning of *Our little lives are kept in equipoise.*

Forces and counterforces keep our lives in equilibrium (delicate balance, harmony).

Our little lives: The solar system in which we reside has a Sun (a star), eight planets, five dwarf planets (Pluto, Ceres, Haumea, Makemake, Eris), 293 moons, approximately 1.4 million asteroids and about 4000 comets. Our solar system is a part of a galaxy (the Milky Way). There are several galaxies. According to a few researchers (for example Camilo Mora) there are around 8.7 million species on earth. How many worlds exist? We do not really know! Therefore, it is appropriate to label our lives as *little lives*. In our day to day life we experience several driving (favourable) and restraining (unfavourable or constraining) forces. A human being might experience turmoil within himself due to the driving forces and resisting forces.

(ii) According to the poet, how are our little lives *kept in equipoise*?

According to the poet, *Our little lives are kept in equipoise*

By opposite attractions and desires;
The struggle of the instinct that enjoys,
And the more noble instinct that aspires.

Conflicting tendencies and desires exist within a person (*opposite attractions and desires*). Human beings might experience desires which seek gratification (immediate gratification) and desires which seek personal growth (mental and spiritual advancement).

As an example, a man might find great comfort and pleasure in sleeping in the morning during the winter months (*instinct that enjoys*). But, there are people who wake up and toil in order to realize their dreams (*more noble instinct that aspires*). A man might find comfort in criticizing (cursing) the system (a system). Satisfaction can also be found in making the world a better place to live in (improving the system/improving a system).

(iii) Give an example which brings out the meaning of *opposite attractions and desires.*

centripetal and centrifugal forces

expansion and contraction

forces of light and darkness

love and hate

pleasure and pain

creative forces (or constructive forces) and destructive forces

(iv) Give an example of an *instinct that enjoys.*

[It is possible to pass in an examination by using unfair means (which may provide temporary or false satisfaction). Studying and passing in an examination is also an option (which provides real joy).

It is possible to find false solace by only imagining and not actually working. It is possible to find true solace by working earnestly.

Idle gossip may provide sadistic pleasure. Spending time in prayer, reading holy books might provide some illumination.]

(v) Give an example of a *more noble instinct that aspires.*

Question 6.

These perturbations, this perpetual jar
Of earthly wants and aspirations high,
Come from the influence of an unseen star,
An undiscovered planet in our sky.

(i) Give the meanings of the following words as they are used in the context of the poem: perturbations, perpetual, jar

(ii) What is a star?

A star is a giant ball of hot gases – mostly hydrogen, some helium and small amounts of other elements. Molecular clouds are large clouds of gas and dust. Stars are formed in molecular clouds.

A star refers to any object that is self-luminous and is sufficiently massive that it can ignite the fusion of elements in its core due to the gravitational pressures inside the object itself.

(iii) What is a planet?

The Greek word planēt means wanderer. A planet

orbits a star,

must be massive enough to have sufficient gravity to force it into a spherical shape.

(iv) What is sky?

Sky is an expanse of space that constitutes an apparent great vault or arch over the earth.

The synonyms of sky are: firmament, welkin.

(v) Explain the meaning of *These perturbations, this . . . our sky.*

Perturbation implies mental disquiet or agitation.

Perpetual implies lasting an indefinitely long time.

Jar implies conflict. Jar also means a discordant sound or combination of sounds.

'Earthly wants' implies mundane satisfiers of needs.

'Aspirations high' refer to lofty objectives.

Unseen star refers to unknown forces (influences beyond our understanding) which influence the life of a human being.

Our sky refers to an infinite cosmic realm beyond our perception.

Longfellow uses cosmic imagery to convey that the conflict between our earthly wants and lofty aspirations are because of unseen, unknown forces.

Question 7.

And as the moon from some dark gate of cloud

Throws o'er the sea a floating bridge of light,

Across whose trembling planks our fancies crowd

Into the realm of mystery and night,–

(i) What is *moon* and what is *cloud* in "*And as the moon from some dark gate of cloud*"?

Moon is a natural satellite of the earth. The time taken by the moon to rotate once on its axis is equal to the time taken by the moon to orbit once around Earth.

A Cloud is the visible aggregate of minute particles of water and/or ice that is formed when water vapour condenses in the atmosphere. Clouds can be of several types, such as, Cirrus, Cirrocumulus, Cirrostratus, Altocumulus, Altostratus, Nimbostratus, Cumulus, Stratocumulus, Stratus, Cumulonimbus, etc.

The Moon reflects light which she receives from the Sun. The clouds might act as an obstruction to moonlight reaching the earth if they cover the moon.

(ii) What sense/feeling is conveyed by "*And as the moon from some dark gate of cloud*"?

"*And as the moon from some dark gate of cloud*" projects an image of the moon emerging from behind dark clouds / a dark cloud. It suggests a moment of illumination/epiphany/revelation after a prolonged period of search for truth. People can be guided by moonlight on a dark night.

(iii) What sense/feeling is conveyed by "*Throws o'er the sea a floating bridge of light*"?

"*Throws o'er the sea a floating bridge of light*" projects the image of a bridge of light which floats over the sea. A 'bridge' helps in connecting two different points. The bridge of light provides a pathway between the known and the unknown.

(iv) What sense/feeling is conveyed by "*Across whose trembling planks our fancies crowd*"?

Planks floating over sea will be wobbly.

The bridge of light provides a path to our thoughts and imaginations.

(v) What sense/feeling is conveyed by "*Into the realm of mystery and night*"?

Deeper truths and facts reside in a different plane.

(vi) Give the meanings of the following words in the context of the poem fancies, realm

____

____

____

Question 8.

So from the world of spirits there descends

A bridge of light, connecting it with this,

O'er whose unsteady floor, that sways and bends,

Wander our thoughts above the dark abyss.

[A dead body might have hands, legs, nose, ears, lungs, kidneys, etc. A living body might also have hands, legs, nose, ears, lungs, kidneys, etc. But, a dead body cannot respond to stimuli. A living body responds to stimuli. A dead body has no feelings and cannot experience pain. What gives energy or life to a body? Some experts have given the name 'spirit' to this energy which gives life to a body.]

(i) Examine the use of the word "*So*" in "*So from the world of spirits there descends*".

In the penultimate stanza of the poem (In the ninth stanza of the poem), Longfellow says,

"*And as the moon from some dark gate of cloud*

Throws o'er the sea a floating bridge of light,

Across whose trembling planks our fancies crowd

Into the realm of mystery and night,–"

H. W. Longfellow continues with the analogy of *bridge of light* in the tenth stanza. Therefore, he begins the tenth stanza with "*So from the world of spirits there descends*".

[penultimate: next to the last]

(ii) What is a spirit? What does "*this*" in "*A bridge of light, connecting it with this*" refer to?

Spirit refers to the soul regarded as separating from the body at death.

In "*A bridge of light, connecting it with this*", "*this*" refers to the world in which human beings live.

(iii) Explain the meaning of "*So from the world of spirits there descends*

A bridge of light, connecting it with this".

A bridge descends from the world of spirits to the world of human beings. The bridge symbolizes a pathway which enables connectivity between the two worlds.

(iv) Explain the meaning of "*O'er whose unsteady floor, that sways and bends*".

The bridge is depicted as unsteady (unstable, shaky), swaying (moving or swinging to and fro) and bending, which implies that we should tread the bridge warily (cautiously) as there can be distractions which might hamper our journey.

(v) Explain the meaning of "*Wander our thoughts above the dark abyss.*"

The word abyss can mean a deep, immeasurable space, a vast chasm or a subterranean ocean. Our thoughts wander above the dark abyss. The bridge of light which descends from the spirit-world to the physical world of human beings might provide a pathway to higher knowledge.

(vi) Is the poem *Haunted Houses* a didactic poem? Support your answer with a reason. [didactic: instructive]

____

____

____

Interesting facts

1. The title of the poem 'Haunted Houses' appears in the second line of the first stanza of the poem.

All houses wherein men have lived and died

Are haunted houses. Through the open doors . . .

2. The second word of the first three lines of the first stanza begins with 'h'.

All houses wherein men have lived and died

Are haunted houses. Through the open doors

The harmless phantoms on their errands glide,

With feet that make no sound upon the floors.

3. The first stanza has *five* words which begin with 'h'.

All houses wherein men have lived and died

Are haunted houses. Through the open doors

The harmless phantoms on their errands glide,

With feet that make no sound upon the floors.

First stanza

4. The fourth stanza and the fifth stanza have *four* words which begin with 'h'.

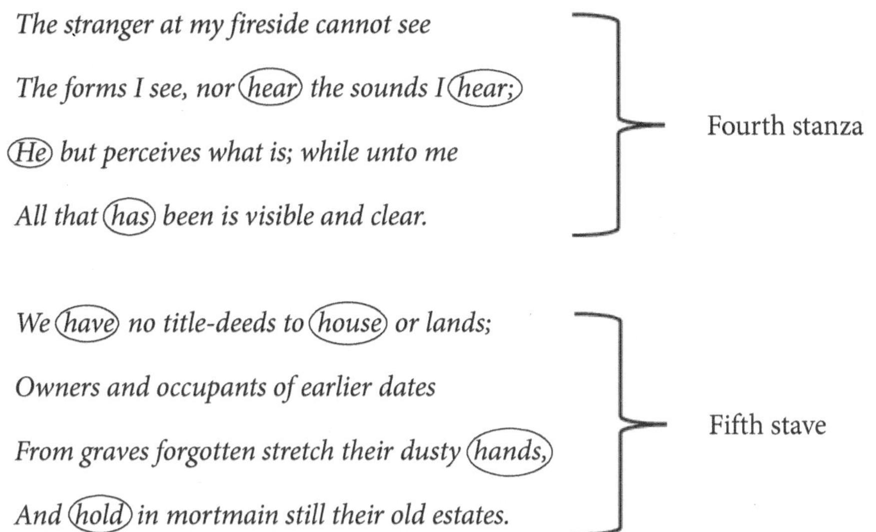

5. The last word of each line of the fifth and tenth staves ends with 's'.

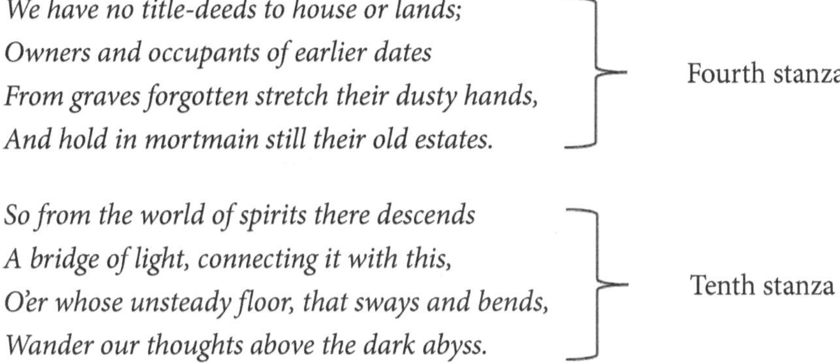

6. The fifth stanza contains two words which end with 'o' and four words which begin with 'O/o'.

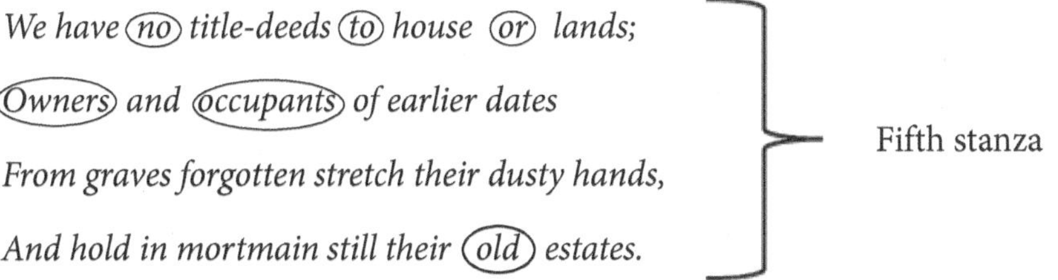

7. The fifth word of the third and fourth lines of the seventh stanza is the same.

Our little lives are kept in equipoise
By opposite attractions and desires;
The struggle of the instinct that enjoys,
And the more noble instinct that aspires.

8. The phrase 'bridge of light' appears in the second line of the ninth and the tenth stanzas. The term "o'er" / "O'er" appears in the second line in the ninth stanza and the third line in the tenth stanza.

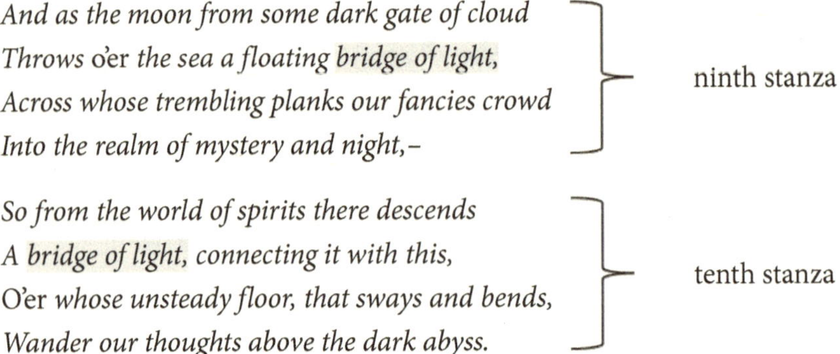

And as the moon from some dark gate of cloud
Throws o'er *the sea a floating bridge of light,*
Across whose trembling planks our fancies crowd
Into the realm of mystery and night,–

ninth stanza

So from the world of spirits there descends
A bridge of light, connecting it with this,
O'er *whose unsteady floor, that sways and bends,*
Wander our thoughts above the dark abyss.

tenth stanza

9. The poem "*Haunted Houses*" is a blend of euphonious poetry and deep philosophy. There is a lilt (rhythmic swing or cadence) in the poem.

The last word of the first line of the poem is '*died*'
The last word of the third line of the poem is '*glide*'

The last word of the second line of the poem is '*doors*'
The last word of the fourth line of the poem is '*floors*'

The last word of the fifth line of the poem is '*stair*'
The last word of the seventh line of the poem is '*air*'

The last word of the sixth line of the poem is '*go*'
The last word of the eighth line of the poem is '*fro*'

The last word of the ninth line of the poem is '*hosts*'
The last word of the eleventh line of the poem is '*ghosts*'

The last word of the tenth line of the poem is '*hall*'
The last word of the twelfth line of the poem is '*wall*'

The last word of the thirteenth line of the poem is '*see*'
The last word of the fifteenth line of the poem is '*me*'

The last word of the fourteenth line of the poem is '*hear*'
The last word of the sixteenth line of the poem is '*clear*'

The last word of the seventeenth line of the poem is '*lands*'
The last word of the nineteenth line of the poem is '*hands*'

The last word of the eighteenth line of the poem is '*dates*'
The last word of the twentieth line of the poem is '*estates*'

The last word of the twenty-first line of the poem is '*sense*'
The last word of the twenty-third line of the poem is '*vapoursdense*'

The last word of the twenty-second line of the poem is '*everywhere*'
The last word of the twenty-fourth line of the poem is '*air*'

The last word of the twenty-fifth line of the poem is '*equipoise*'
The last word of the twenty-seventh line of the poem is '*enjoys*'

The last word of the twenty-sixth line of the poem is '*desires*'
The last word of the twenty-eighth line of the poem is '*aspires*'

The last word of the twenty-ninth line of the poem is '*jar*'
The last word of the thirty-first line of the poem is '*star*'

The last word of the thirtieth line of the poem is '*high*'
The last word of the thirty-second line of the poem is '*sky*'

The last word of the thirty-third line of the poem is '*cloud*'
The last word of the thirty-fifth line of the poem is '*crowd*'

The last word of the thirty-fourth line of the poem is '*light*'
The last word of the thirty-sixth line of the poem is '*night*'

The last word of the thirty-seventh line of the poem is '*descends*'
The last word of the thirty-ninth line of the poem is '*bends*'

The last word of the thirty-eighth line of the poem is '*this*'
The last word of the fortieth line of the poem is '*abyss*'

10. The poem presents an idea of life and afterlife. Longfellow through his poem *Haunted Houses* projects his belief in the existence and proximity of spiritual beings.

11. The tenth stanza contains *seven* words which end with 's'.

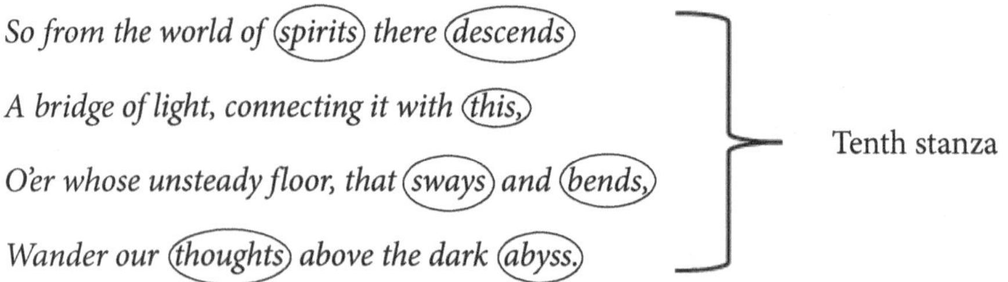

Multiple choice questions

(i) According to the poet, __________ are haunted houses.
(a) all houses wherein men have lived and died
(b) some of the houses wherein men have lived and died
(c) most of the houses wherein men have lived and died
(d) none of the houses wherein men have lived and died

(ii) According to the poet
(a) the guests and the hosts at table are equal in number
(b) there are less guests at table than the hosts

(c) there are more guests at table than the hosts

(d) it cannot be ascertained whether the number of guests at table are more than the hosts or less than the hosts

(iii) According to the poet, the stranger at his fireside
(a) can see the forms that the poet is able to see but cannot hear the sounds which the poet is able to hear
(b) cannot see the forms that the poet is able to see but can hear the sounds which the poet is able to hear
(c) cannot see the forms that the poet is able to see and cannot hear the sounds which the poet is able to hear
(d) can see the forms which the poet is able to see and can hear the sounds which the poet is able to hear

(iv) According to the poet, the stranger at his fireside
(a) can see the forms that the poet is not able to see but cannot hear the sounds which the poet is able to hear
(b) cannot see the forms that the poet is able to see but can hear the sounds which the poet is not able to hear
(c) can see the forms that the poet is not able to see and can hear the sounds which the poet is not able to hear
(d) cannot see the forms which the poet is able to see and cannot hear the sounds which the poet is able to hear

(v) "dusty hands" symbolize
(a) hands of living human beings
(b) hands of the deceased owners and occupants of earlier dates
(c) hands of construction workers
(d) hands of vegetable sellers

(vi) According to the poet, our little lives are
(a) not kept in equipoise due to opposite attractions and desires
(b) not kept in equipoise due to same attractions and desires
(c) kept in equipoise by opposite attractions and desires
(d) kept in equipoise by similar attractions and desires

(vii) According to the poem, our little lives are kept in equipoise by
(a) joy and suffering
(b) same attractions and desires
(c) wealth and health
(d) opposite attractions and desires.

(viii) According to the poet which instinct is more noble
(a) the instinct that enjoys
(b) the instinct that aspires
(c) the instinct that both enjoys and aspires
(d) the instinct that neither enjoys nor aspires

(ix) The poem *Haunted Houses* contains a reference to (a/an)
(a) White Dwarfs
(b) Neutron Star
(c) Red Dwarfs
(d) unseen star

(x) The poem *Haunted Houses* contains a reference to (an)
(a) gas giants
(b) small, rocky planets
(c) terrestrial planets
(d) undiscovered planet

Cues

(i) – (a) (ii) – (c) (iii) – (c) (iv) – (d) (v) – (b) (vi) – (c)
(vii) – (d) (viii) – (b) (ix) – (d) (x) – (d)

Question. Explain each stanza of H. W. Longfellow's poem *Haunted Houses.*

All houses wherein men have lived and died *Are haunted houses. Through the open doors* *The harmless phantoms on their errands glide,* *With feet that make no sound upon the floors.*	All the houses in which the people have lived and died are haunted houses. The departed live in our memories and thus are a part of our lives and our homes. The souls of the departed share our living spaces. All houses in which people have lived and died are haunted by the memories and presence of those people who once inhabited the houses.
We meet them at the door way, on the stair, *Along the passages they come and go,* *Impalpable impressions on the air,* *A sense of something moving to and fro.*	
There are more guests at table than the hosts *Invited; the illuminated hall* *Is thronged with quiet, inoffensive ghosts,* *As silent as the pictures on the wall.*	A simile is a figure of speech which compares two dissimilar things. Terms such as *like* or *as* might appear in a simile. The third stanza contains a simile: *inoffensive ghosts,* *As silent as the pictures on the wall.*
The stranger at my fireside cannot see *The forms I see, nor hear the sounds I hear;* *He but perceives what is; while unto me* *All that has been is visible and clear.*	fireside is also called hearthside.

We have no title-deeds to house or lands; *Owners and occupants of earlier dates* *From graves forgotten stretch their dusty hands,* *And hold in mortmain still their old estates.*	We do not own the title-deeds to house or land. The stanza captures the fleetingness of life and the human desire to hold on to possessions. Owners and occupants of earlier dates refers to the preceding generation who lived before the current generation. Owners of the previous generation owned the title-deeds. The influence and legacy of the past generations continue to affect the present.
The spirit-world around this world of sense *Floats like an atmosphere, and everywhere* *Wafts through these earthly mists and vapoursdense* *A vital breath of more ethereal air.*	The spirit-world floats like an atmosphere around the world of sense.
Our little lives are kept in equipoise *By opposite attractions and desires;* *The struggle of the instinct that enjoys,* *And the more noble instinct that aspires.*	Our lives are kept in equilibrium by opposite attractions and desires. [Every man experiences one pain in his life: either the pain of discipline or the pain of regret. Devoting an hour each day for studying biology requires discipline. Watching a two-hour movie might provide relaxation. A human being has a choice: study or relax.]

These perturbations, this perpetual jar *Of earthly wants and aspirations high,* *Come from the influence of an unseen star,* *An undiscovered planet in our sky.* (Do the celestial bodies influence our lives?)	The planet Uranus was identified by William Herschel in 1781. The astronomers discovered irregularities in the orbit of Uranus. The effects due to gravity of a more distant planet could explain these perturbances. Johann Gottfried Galle confirmed the existence of planet Neptune on the night of September 23-24, 1846. Urbain Jean-Joseph Le Verrier and John Couch Adams (working independently) had calculated the location of planet Neptune.
And as the moon from some dark gate of cloud *Throws o'er the sea a floating bridge of light,* *Across whose trembling planks our fancies crowd* *Into the realm of mystery and night,–*	
So from the world of spirits there descends *A bridge of light, connecting it with this,* *O'er whose unsteady floor, that sways and bends,* *Wander our thoughts above the dark abyss.* (Is our sense of connection with the world an illusory one?)	*world of spirits* might refer to invisible spiritual intelligences. Our thoughts might be governed by higher intelligence, which might guide, strengthen and console us. Our thoughts wander across this unsteady bridge into the enigma of the unknown.

Longfellow's *Haunted Houses* is characterized by clarity and precision; equilibrium and fluidity.

An interesting verse in John Milton's *Paradise Lost, Book IV, [The Argument]*:

Millions of spiritual creatures walk the Earth
Unseen, both when we wake, and when we sleep:

H. W. Longfellow in his poem *Haunted Houses* says:

All houses wherein men have lived and died
Are haunted houses.

T. S. Eliot's poem *The Waste Land* is an interesting poem having five parts: The Burial of the Dead, A Game of Chess, The Fire Sermon, Death by Water, What the Thunder Said. An interesting stanza from the fifth part of the poem is:

Who is the third who walks always beside you?
When I count, there are only you and I together
But when I look ahead up the white road
There is always another one walking beside you
Gliding wrapt in a brown mantle, hooded
I do not know whether a man or a woman
—But who is that on the other side of you?

Who is the *third* who walks always beside you?

Who is the extra member present? Is it a spirit?

[Does the poem *Haunted Houses* explore a spectrum ranging from the known to the unknown, material to the non-material, the physical to the spiritual?]

The ninth stanza contains an interesting phrase: *And as the moon from some dark gate of cloud.* A few important terms related to clouds are detailed below:

nephogram: a photograph of a cloud or clouds

nephograph: an instrument for photographing clouds

nephology: a branch of meteorology dealing with clouds

nephometer: an instrument for measuring the amount of cloud cover in the sky

nephoscope: an instrument for determining the altitude of clouds and the velocity and direction of their motion.

okta: a unit used in meteorology to measure cloud cover, equivalent to a cloud cover of one eighth of the sky.

[Wallace's note: There are several systems, structures, and layers. There must be a link between systems, structures, layers and the levels of consciousness of the mind. With dedication and perseverance these links can be discovered to some extent and they may provide new insights.]

The Glove and the Lions

– Leigh Hunt

The author of this workbook retrieved the poem *The Glove and the Lions* from https://www.public-domain-poetry.com/james-henry-leigh-hunt/glove-and-the-lions-457 on July 28, 2024 at 1543 hours

King Francis was a hearty king, and loved a royal sport,
And one day as his lions fought, sat looking on the court;
The nobles filled the benches, and the ladies in their pride,
And 'mongst them sat the Count de Lorge, with one for whom he sighed:
And truly 'twas a gallant thing to see that crowning show,
Valour and love, and a king above, and the royal beasts below.

Ramped and roared the lions, with horrid laughing jaws;
They bit, they glared, gave blows like beams, a wind went with their paws;
With wallowing might and stifled roar they rolled on one another;
Till all the pit with sand and mane was in a thunderous smother;
The bloody foam above the bars came whisking through the air;
Said Francis then, "Faith, gentlemen, we're better here than there."

De Lorge's love o'erheard the King, a beauteous lively dame
With smiling lips and sharp bright eyes, which always seemed the same;
She thought, the Count my lover is brave as brave can be;
He surely would do wondrous things to show his love of me;
King, ladies, lovers, all look on; the occasion is divine;
I'll drop my glove, to prove his love; great glory will be mine.

She dropped her glove, to prove his love, then looked at him and smiled;
He bowed, and in a moment leaped among the lions wild:
The leap was quick, return was quick, he has regained his place,
Then threw the glove, but not with love, right in the lady's face.
"By God!" said Francis, "rightly done!" and he rose from where he sat:
"No love," quoth he, "but vanity, sets love a task like that."

Word		**Meaning**
hearty	:	warm-hearted, affectionate
royal	:	established or chartered by or existing under the patronage of a sovereign
nobles	:	of, belonging to, or constituting a hereditary class possessing special social or political status in a country or state
pride	:	splendor
gallant	:	stately, grand
Valour	:	boldness or determination in facing great danger
ramp	:	(of a lion) to rise on the hind legs, (of a lion) stand on the hind legs
Ramped	:	leaped with fury, dashed with fury
horrid	:	dreadful
glare	:	a fiercely or angrily piercing stare
glared	:	stared angrily
wallow	:	to roll about in mud
stifled	:	smothered
pit	:	a naturally formed or excavated hole or cavity in the ground
mane	:	the long hair growing on the back of or about the neck and neighboring parts of lion
smother	:	envelop
bar	:	a relatively long, evenly shaped piece of some solid substance, as metal or wood, used as a guard or obstruction

whisk	:	to move with a rapid, sweeping stroke
overhear	:	to hear (speech or a speaker) without the speaker's intention or knowledge
dame	:	the official title of a female member of the Order of the British Empire
glove	:	a covering for the hand made with a separate sheath for each finger and for the thumb
quoth	:	said (the word *quoth* is always placed before the subject)
vanity	:	excessive pride in one's appearance, qualities, abilities, achievements, etc.,

Punctuation marks statistics

Number of apostrophes: 07
Number of commas: 35
Number of semi-colons: 13
Number of colons: 03
Number of full-stops (period symbols): 05
Number of exclamation marks: 02
Number of dashes: 00
Number of hyphens: 00
Number of opening inverted commas: 05
Number of closing inverted commas: 05

The poem can be very helpful in conveying the fact that some people can play dangerous games (de Lorge's love played a dangerous game). The poem helps the reader understand the concepts of *love* and *vanity*.

The first stanza introduces King Francis who loves a royal sport (lions fighting with each other) and Count de Lorge who is in love with a girl (who is also watching the lions fighting with each other). Along with the King, the nobles and the ladies also are spectators of the grand fight amongst the lions.

The first and the second stanza of the poem help the reader in visualizing a pit (which is either a naturally occurring pit or a pit which is especially dug out) where the lions fight with each other and the spectators sitting above are able to obtain a clear view. The pit is surrounded by bars (*The bloody foam above the bars came whisking through the air*) which ensures that the lions will not be able to attack the spectators.

King Francis remarked, "*Faith, gentlemen, we're better here than there.*" The lady whom de Lorge loved overheard Francis' statement and was overcome with a desire to exhibit to the king and the nobility how deep de Lorge's love was for her. She dropped her glove into the pit of lions and looked and smiled at de Lorge. de Lorge bowed to her, quickly descended into the pit, retrieved the glove, and came out from the pit, and then threw the glove (not with love) right in the lady's face.

King Francis laconic statement, "No love, but vanity, sets love a task like that" explains that the self-interests of the lady outweighed her love for de Lorge.

The poem is a treatise on deep thinking, quick thinking, self-esteem, quick action, judgment and ulterior motives. The poem outlines a method of responding in a difficult situation.

Types of love

Eros: passionate love
Philia: shared goodwill
Storge: familial love
Agape: universal love
Ludus: playful or uncommitted love
Pragma: practical love founded in reason
Philautia: self-love

Vanity

Vanity is used to describe something that is done with the aim of getting praise, fame, or approval (*I'll drop my glove, to prove his love; great glory will be mine*) rather than for serious or good reasons. Vanity might be considered as a weakness.

Critical analysis

Jumping into a pit in which lions are present or a pit in which lions are fighting each other can be precarious (perilous). The lions might tear a person apart.

The lady whom Count de Lorge sighed for knew that de Lorge will be able to jump into the pit of lions and come out alive (unharmed) of the pit.

de Lorge knew fully well that he would be able to retrieve the glove from the pit in which lions were fighting each other.

The lady threw her glove in the pit of lions. This action of the lady was not correct.

de Lorge retrieved the glove from the pit. He proved that he was not frightened of lions. He proved that he was quick. He proved that he could face dangers. He threw the glove (but not with love) at the lady's face. He understood the ulterior motives of the lady. de Lorge was able to discern the motives of the lady he admired.

King Francis remarked, "*By God! rightly done!*" and stood up. Thus, de Lorge received a standing ovation from the king.

King Francis' sagacious statement "No love, but vanity, sets love a task like that" helps the reader in comprehending that the lady was yearning for adulation.

The poem delivers an important message that we (human beings) need to develop and use our ability to discern. The poem is a treatise on risk management (risk analysis).

James Henry Leigh Hunt (October 19, 1784 - 1859)

James Henry Leigh Hunt was born to Isaac and Mary Shewell Hunt. Leight Hunt was an essayist and a journalist as well as a prolific poet. Leigh Hunt was a virtuoso (a person who has special knowledge or skill in a field) of atmosphere and mood. Leigh Hunt was married to Marianne Kent.

Major works:

Juvenilia

Foliage

Sir Ralph Esher

Read the extracts given below and answer the questions that follow:

Question 1.

King Francis was a hearty king, and loved a royal sport,
And one day as his lions fought, sat looking on the court;
The nobles filled the benches, and the ladies in their pride,
And 'mongst them sat the Count de Lorge, with one for whom he sighed:
And truly 'twas a gallant thing to see that crowning show,
Valour and love, and a king above, and the royal beasts below.

['mongst: amongst
'twas: contraction of *it was.*]

(i) Examine the significance of "*King Francis was a hearty king*".

The word '*hearty*' has several meanings: (i) cordial, (ii) jovial, (iii) enthusiastic, (iv) physically vigorous, (v) affectionate, (vi) genuine.

If we interpret *hearty* as 'physically vigorous' or 'strong and well', then the phrase *King Francis was a hearty king* helps the reader comprehend his (King Francis') liking for the sport of lions fighting with each other.

If we interpret *hearty* as 'jovial', then the phrase *King Francis was a hearty king* helps the reader comprehend (or appreciate) that although King Francis was of jovial nature even then the act of a lady throwing her glove into the enclosure where lions were fighting each other only to prove her lover's (de Lorge's) love had such an impact on him that he remarked, "No love, but vanity, sets love a task like that."

(ii) How is de Lorge's love described in the poem?
de Lorge's love is described as a beauteous lively dame with smiling lips and sharp bright eyes, which always seemed the same.
The girl who is de Lorge's love, is however, afflicted with vanity.

(iii) How are lions described in the poem?
Ramped and roared the lions, with horrid laughing jaws;
They bit, they glared, gave blows like beams, a wind went with their paws;
With wallowing might and stifled roar they rolled on one another;
The lions are described as *wild* (*He bowed, and in a moment leaped among the lions wild*).

(iv) Explain the meaning of "*the ladies in their pride*".
"*the ladies in their pride*" implies the ladies were in their splendor.
"*the ladies in their pride*" implies the ladies were in all magnificence.
lady: a polite term for any woman; a woman of good family or social position

(v) Who is a Count?
A Count (in some European countries) is a nobleman equivalent in rank to an English earl.

(vi) Explain the meaning of "*with one for whom he sighed*".
Count de Lorge was sitting with the girl he admired/wooed.

(vii) What is the difference between valour and love?
valour: heroic courage
love: a feeling of warm personal attachment or deep affection.

(viii) What is the difference between love and vanity?
vanity: conceit, lack of real value.
Love is patient, love is kind.
Love does not envy, love does not boast, love is not proud.
Love does not dishonor others, love is not self-seeking, love is not easily angered, love keeps no record of wrongs. Love does not delight in evil but rejoices with the truth. Love always protects, always trusts, always hopes, always perseveres.

Question 2.

Ramped and roared the lions, with horrid laughing jaws;
They bit, they glared, gave blows like beams, a wind went with their paws;
With wallowing might and stifled roar they rolled on one another;
Till all the pit with sand and mane was in a thunderous smother;
The bloody foam above the bars came whisking through the air;
Said Francis then, "Faith, gentlemen, we're better here than there."

[Today, there are laws which prohibit animal fighting ventures that are related to commerce or human entertainment. In our country, an Act, *The Prevention of Cruelty to Animals Act, 1960* has been enacted.]

(i) Which are the terms used in the first stanza of the poem for describing the fight amongst the lions?
royal sport, And one day as his lions fought, crowning show

(ii) Explain the meaning of "*Ramped and roared the lions*".

Ramped: the lions rose or stood on their hind legs; the lions leapt or dashed at each other with fury.

Roared: uttered a loud, deep cry.

(iii) Explain the meaning of "*They bit, they glared, gave blows like beams, a wind went with their paws*".

'*They bit*' implies the lions were cutting, wounding or tearing at each other with their teeth.

'*they glared*' implies that the lions were angrily staring at each other.

A *beam* refers to any of various relatively long pieces of metal, wood, stone, etc. which can be used as rigid members.

'*gave blows like beams*' implies that the lions were hitting each other with great force.

'*a wind went with their paws*' indicates the great force with which the lions were hitting each other.

Wind is air in motion.

(iv) Explain the meaning of "*With wallowing might and stifled roar they rolled on one another*". What is the significance of the term '*stifled roar*'?

Wallow implies to roll about.

A male lion can weigh around 190 kg and the weight of a female can be around 126 kg. The weight of a lion (or lioness) is an indicator of the pressure which it can exert.

Stifled implies suffocated or to suffer from difficulty in breathing. The lions were attacking each other so aggressively that they were suffocating each other hence their roar was stifled roar.

(v) Explain the meaning of "*Till all the pit with sand and mane was in a thunderous smother*".

Mane refers to the long hair growing on the back of or about the neck of a lion. Smother means to stifle or suffocate.
It is easy to visualize the lions attacking each other very fiercely causing terror and dread. The pit is turned into a cloud of dust, sand and mane because of the lions fighting with each other.

(vi) Explain the meaning of "*The bloody foam above the bars came whisking through the air*".
The bloody foam because of the lions fighting with each other flung into the air.

(vii) Give the meanings of the following words in the context of the stanza:

horrid, jaws, beams, wallowing, stifled, thunderous, smother, foam, whisking

____

____

____

Question 3.

De Lorge's love o'erheard the King, a beauteous lively dame
With smiling lips and sharp bright eyes, which always seemed the same;
She thought, the Count my lover is brave as brave can be;
He surely would do wondrous things to show his love of me;
King, ladies, lovers, all look on; the occasion is divine;
I'll drop my glove, to prove his love; great glory will be mine.

[*de*: used in French and Spanish personal names (for example, Jean de La Fontaine), originally to indicate place of origin.]

(i) Account for the presence of de Lorge's love?

King Francis loved a royal sport – wild savage lions fighting each other. One day King Francis, his courtiers, noblemen and ladies were watching the ferocious lions fighting each other in the enclosure below. Count de Lorge and the lady the Count sighed for were also watching the *crowning show*.

(ii) What did de Lorge's love overhear?

de Lorge's love overheard King Francis' remark, "*Faith, gentlemen, we're better here than there.*"

(iii) What did de Lorge's love do *to prove his love* for her?

When De Lorge's love overheard the King's statement, "*Faith, gentlemen, we're better here than there*", she fancied (pictured) that she would show the king and the nobility present along with the king how devoted her lover was to her. She, therefore, dropped her glove in the enclosure (pit) where the lions were ferociously fighting each other. She then looked at de Lorge and smiled at him.

(iv) How did De Lorge respond to his love's action?

De Lorge bowed, and in a moment leaped among the lions wild. De Lorge retrieved the glove and came back to his place very quickly (without losing time). He then threw the glove, but not with love, right in the lady's face.

(v) What inferences pertaining to the personality of the person whom de Lorge sighed for can you draw from the poem from which the above stanza is extracted?

The lady who de Lorge sighed for was looking for adulation. She wanted to exhibit that her lover would do anything for her. She allowed pride and vanity to dictate her actions in a romantic relationship.

Question 4.

She dropped her glove, to prove his love, then looked at him and smiled;
He bowed, and in a moment leaped among the lions wild:
The leap was quick, return was quick, he has regained his place,
Then threw the glove, but not with love, right in the lady's face.
"By God!" said Francis, "rightly done!" and he rose from where he sat:
"No love," quoth he, "but vanity, sets love a task like that."

(i) Whom does "*She*" in "*She dropped her glove*" refer to? Whom does "*him*" in "*. . . then looked at him and smiled*" refer to?

____

____

____

(ii) What is a *glove*?

____

____

____

(iii) Give an example of imagery and simile from Hunt's poem '*The Glove and the Lions*'.

____

____

____

(iv) Critically evaluate the actions of (a) the lady de Lorge pined for, (b) de Lorge.

____

____

____

(v) Explain the meaning of *"No love," quoth he, "but vanity, sets love a task like that."*

____

____

____

Interesting facts

1. The name of the King (Francis) appears in the first stanza, second stanza and the fourth stanza of the poem.

2. The name of the Count (de Lorge) appears in the first stanza and the third stanza of the poem.

3. The Word '*royal*' appears in the first line and the sixth line of the poem.

4. The word '*love*' appears in the first stanza, third stanza and the fourth stanza of the poem. The word '*love*' appears in the sixth line, thirteenth line, sixteenth line, eighteenth line, nineteenth line, twenty-second line and the twenty-fourth line of the poem.

5. The phrase '*his love*' appears in the sixteenth line, eighteenth line and nineteenth line of the poem.

6. The phrase '*to prove his love*' appears in the third stanza and the fourth stanza of the poem.

7. Three words which begin with '*w*' appear consecutively in the eighth line of the poem

They bit, they glared, gave blows like beams, a wind went with their paws;

8. Four words which begin with '*s*' appear in the fourteenth line of the poem

With smiling lips and sharp bright eyes, which always seemed the same;

9. The word '*brave*' appears twice in fifteenth line:

She thought, the Count my lover is brave as brave can be;

10. The word '*quick*' appears twice in the twenty-first line:

The leap was quick, return was quick, he has regained his place,

11. The word '*love*' appears twice in the twenty-fourth line:

"No love," quoth he, "but vanity, sets love a task like that."

12. The word '*glove*' appears thrice in the poem (excluding the title).

13. The word '*lions*' appears thrice in the poem (excluding the title).

Multiple choice questions

(i) ______________ is the King in the poem *The Glove and the Lions*

(a) James

(b) John

(c) Andrew

(d) Francis

(ii) According to the poem, *The Glove and the Lions*, King Francis was a ______________ king.

(a) belligerent

(b) hearty

(c) misanthrope

(d) philanthropist

(iii) According to the poem *The Glove and the Lions*, King Francis ______________ a royal sport.

(a) loved

(b) hated

(c) was indifferent to

(d) banned

(iv) The 'royal sport' mentioned in *The Glove and the Lions* is ______________

(a) bull-fight

(b) fight of lions with men

(c) fight amongst the tigers

(d) fight amongst the lions

(v) ______________ is the Count in the poem *The Glove and the Lions*

(a) de Francis

(b) de Augustine

(c) Philip

(d) de Lorge

(vi) Count de Lorge's love overheard the ______________

(a) Count

(b) King

(c) courtier

(d) attendant

(vii) Count de Lorge's love dropped her ______________ in the pit in which the lions were fighting each other.

(a) sandal

(b) bangle

(c) glove

(d) ear-ring

Cues

(i) – (d) (ii) – (b) (iii) – (a) (iv) – (d) (v) – (d)

(vi) – (b) (vii) – (c)

Application of knowledge

Harry Ingham and Joseph Luft presented the Johari window (in 1955) which is detailed below:

	Known to self	Not known to self
Known to others	I Area of Free Activity	II Blind Area
Not known to others	III Avoided or Hidden Area	IV Area of Unknown Activity

Quadrant I refers to behavior and motivation known to others and known to self.
Quadrant II represents what others can see in ourselves of which we are unaware.
Quadrant III represents what we know but do not reveal to others.
Quadrant IV represents the behavior and motivation of which neither the individual is aware nor others are aware.

Question. What did the lady whom Count de Lorge pined for know about Count de Lorge?

____

____

____

Question. What did Count de Lorge know about himself which the girl whom he pined for did not know?

____

____

____

Question. What did Count de Lorge know about himself and the girl whom he pined for also knew?

____

____

____

Question. What can be the effects of emotional deprivation on an individual?

____

____

____

[Some people are really experts in playing dirty mind games. They can convince a person of their sincerity while manipulating the person like a puppet-master. They might fool a person by appearing to be honest, generous and helping while in their heart of hearts they are just waiting for the moment to implement their wicked scheme(s). Some men (who appear to be calm and gentle) might take advantage / try to take advantage of girls, by playing dirty mind games. A number of cybercriminals play mind games with other innocent, gullible computer users. There are people on this planet who earn a lot of money by selling God/religion. Some teachers and/or students might play mind games in an academic classroom.]

When Great Trees Fall

– Maya Angelou

[Wallace's note: The poem *When Great Trees Fall* appears to be free of poetic formalities.]

Assume that you are weak in Physics (subject) and you have to appear for an All-India competitive exam (which has Physics as one of the compulsory subjects). A tutor starts teaching you Physics in such a way that you are able to understand the subject and you start loving the subject. Assume that no other person can teach you Physics akin to your Physics tutor. Your Physics tutor has covered fifty percent of the syllabus and then he dies. How would you feel? You might feel sad and lost (like a rudderless ship). After some time, you might continue studying Physics but you might miss the guidance of your tutor who is not alive now. Now read Maya Angelou's poem *When Great Trees Fall.* The poem details the vicissitudes a person encounters in life after losing a truly great person/truly great persons.

A few interesting points related to the poem:

1. When great trees fall,

Third character of *When*: *e*
Third character of *great*: *e*
Third character of *trees*: *e*

2. rocks on distant hills shudder,

Second character of *distant*: *i*
Second character of *hills*: *i*

3. lions hunker down

The second character of each word in the third line is a vowel:
Second character of *lions*: *i*
Second character of *hunker*: *u*
Second character of *down*: *o*

4. First line of first stanza: *When great trees fall,*

First line of second stanza: *When great trees fall*
First line of third stanza: *When great souls die,*
First line of fourth stanza: *Great souls die and*
First line of the last stanza: *And when great souls die,*

5. James Baldwin was an essayist, novelist and a playwright. James Baldwin was born on August 02, 1924 and passed into ages on December 01, 1987. According to some authorities, Maya Angelou penned the poem "*When Great Trees Fall*" after the death of James Baldwin and recited it at Baldwin's funeral.

The poem *When Great Trees Fall* is timeless and prescient. It helps the reader and the listener develop unbending commitment through its message: *Be and be better*. The poem is psychologically penetrating.

6. Martin Luther King, Jr. led the civil rights movement in the United States from the mid-1950s until his death. Martin Luther King, Jr. died on April 04, 1968.

Word		Meaning
shudder	:	to tremble with a sudden convulsive movement, as from horror, fear, or cold
hunker	:	to squat on one's heels
lumber	:	to move clumsily or heavily, especially from great or ponderous bulk
recoil	:	to draw back; start or shrink back, as in alarm, horror, or disgust
eroded	:	eaten out or away
beyond	:	on or to the farther side of
sterile	:	not productive of results, ideas, etc.
clarity	:	pellucidity
gnaw	:	to wear away or remove by persistent biting or nibbling
wizened	:	withered
radiance	:	radiant brightness or light
bloom	:	a flourishing, healthy condition
soothing	:	bringing tranquility, calm, ease, or comfort
vibration	:	rhythmic and steady to and fro movement

Punctuation marks statistics

Number of commas: 28
Number of period symbols: 18

Maya Angelou (04 April 1928 – 28 May 2014)

Maya Angelou (Marguerite Annie Johnson) was a celebrated American activist, autobiographer, poet and storyteller. She was an actress, composer, dancer, director, educator and singer. Angelou was conferred with the National Medal of Arts (by President Bill Clinton, in 2000 AD) and Presidential Medal of Freedom (by President Barack Obama in 2010).

Major works:

I Know Why the Caged Bird Sings (1969)
Singin' and Swingin' and Gettin' Merry Like Christmas (1976)
Mrs. Flowers: A Moment of Friendship (1986)
A Song Flung up to Heaven (2002)

(i) What does the poet say in the first stanza of the poem *When Great Trees Fall*?

The poem *When Great Trees Fall* opens with a metaphor "*When great trees fall*" which symbolizes the passing away of a legend/prodigy/truly great person/influential person/loved person. It is difficult to measure the impact of a great tree falling down. The loss suffered because of a great tree falling is immeasurable, irreparable and perhaps irreversible. The first stanza of the poem explains that when great trees fall the rocks on distant hills shudder, the lions hunker down in tall grasses and even elephants lumber after safety. The death of a great person leaves behind a void which cannot be filled. People may experience waves of intense and very difficult emotions, profound sadness and grief, despair, helplessness, trauma and shock. The effect of the deaths of truly great persons is felt far and wide (*rocks on distant hills shudder*). Lion is a fearless apex predator. Elephants are the largest land mammals. But when great trees fall even the lions hunker down in tall grasses and elephants lumber after safety.

[According to some experts, death is the separation of body from soul. The death of an important person can be painful to the people left behind.]

(ii) What does the poet say in the second stanza of the poem *When Great Trees Fall*?

The second stanza opens with a metaphor "*When great trees fall in forests*".

When great trees fall in forests the small things recoil into silence and their senses are eroded beyond fear. This could imply that even children feel the pain when great people die. It could also imply that the people who are not well-known feel the pain when great people die. The pain is so intense that children and people who are unknown recoil into silence. They are not able to speak.

(iii) What does the poet say in the third stanza of the poem *When Great Trees Fall*?

Loss of great souls refers to the death of people who were close to us, nurtured us and had a lasting impact on us.

When great souls die the air around us becomes light, rare and sterile. We breathe briefly. Our eyes are able to see with hurtful clarity the value of the person(s) we have lost. Our memory is suddenly sharpened and regrets the kind words unsaid and the promised walks never taken. These memories gnaw on us.

(iv) What does the poet say in the fourth stanza of the poem *When Great Trees Fall*?

When great souls die they take away a part of our shared reality with them. Their presence and guidance shaped our understanding. Now that they are no more, we feel diminished. Our thoughts, our judgments are influenced and shaped by the brilliance of great souls. When these great souls leave for their permanent abode we lose guidance and direction which leads to a sense of loss. We can feel anxious, troubled or angry when great souls die but the death of great souls also leaves us in a state of profound ignorance and despair ("*dark, cold caves*"). The death of great souls affects the intellectual fabric of the society.

(v) What does the poet say in the fifth stanza of the poem *When Great Trees Fall*?

The fifth stanza helps the reader transition from the feelings of emptiness and loss towards hope. When great souls die then after a period, peace blooms slowly and always irregularly. The pain and sorrow of losing a loved one may never leave us, yet, the memory of the loved one will continue to affect and shape our lives. We can be. Be and be better for great souls existed.

After the intense angst and disruption caused by the death of influential figures, a sense of peace eventually emerges. With the passage of time, the void left due to the death of the great souls is filled with a stirring energy. Our senses begin to heal although they have been altered by the death of great people. The legacy left behind by the great people serves as a beacon for us.

Read the following extracts from Maya Angelou's poem '*When Great Trees Fall*' and answer the questions that follow:

Question 1.

When great trees fall,
rocks on distant hills shudder,
lions hunker down
in tall grasses,
and even elephants
lumber after safety.

(i) What is a tree?

A tree is a perennial plant having a permanent, woody, self-supporting main stem or trunk, ordinarily growing to a considerable height, and usually developing branches at some distance from the ground.

Trees can be divided into a few categories, for example, deciduous trees and evergreen trees. Trees may belong to the angiosperm group or the gymnosperm group.

[There are many important lessons which can be learnt from the lexis of silence of the active lives of trees. Trees provides nutrients while they are alive. After a great tree has fallen down, it provides firewood and furniture.]

(ii) What is a rock? What is a hill?
A rock is mineral matter of various composition, consolidated or unconsolidated, assembled in masses or considerable quantities in nature, as by the action of heat or water.
Rocks are commonly divided into three major classes: igneous rocks, sedimentary rocks, and metamorphic rocks.
A hill is a natural elevation of the earth's surface, smaller than a mountain.

Petrology : the study of rocks.
Orology: study of mountains.

(iii) Give two examples of tall grasses?
A few examples of tall grasses are: Frost Grass, 'Northwind' Switch Grass, Pennisetum glaucum 'Purple Majesty' Ornamental Millet, Zebra Grass, Hardy Clumping Bamboo, Pampas Grass.

(iv) Give the meanings of the following words in the context of the stanza:

shudder, hunker, lumber

___

___

___

(v) According to the poem, what effect does falling of 'great trees' in forests have on small things?

When great trees fall
in forests,
small things recoil into silence,
their senses
eroded beyond fear.

Question 2.

When great trees fall
in forests,
small things recoil into silence,
their senses
eroded beyond fear.

[Some of the effects of the falling of 'great trees' are detailed in the first two stanzas of the poem:

When great trees fall,
rocks on distant hills shudder,
lions hunker down
in tall grasses,
and even elephants
lumber after safety.

When great trees fall
in forests,
small things recoil into silence,
their senses
eroded beyond fear.]

(i) According to the poem what effect does falling of 'great trees' have on rocks?

(ii) According to the poem what effect does falling of 'great trees' have on lions?

(iii) According to the poem what effect does falling of 'great trees' have on elephants?

(iv) What is Maya Angelou's intention of using the metaphor of a tree falling in the jungle and its effect on the fauna?

Maya Angelou uses the metaphor of a tree falling in the forest and its effect on the fauna for describing the enormity of death and the impact of death on those struggling to cope in its aftermath.

(v) What is the central message of Maya Angelou's poem '*When Great Trees Fall*'?

The poem progresses beyond the vacuum (emptiness) and sense of loss (caused by death) to offer hope for healing

And when great souls die,
after a period peace blooms,
slowly and always
irregularly. Spaces fill
with a kind of
soothing electric vibration.
Our senses, restored, never
to be the same, whisper to us.
They existed. They existed.
We can be. Be and be
better. For they existed.

(vi) What is a forest?

Forest refers to an area that has a large number of trees. Various animals live in a forest. The prominent types of forests are: temperate forests, tropical forests and boreal forests.

Question 3.

When great souls die,
the air around us becomes
light, rare, sterile.
We breathe, briefly.
Our eyes, briefly,
see with
a hurtful clarity.
Our memory, suddenly sharpened,
examines,
gnaws on kind words

unsaid,
promised walks
never taken.

(i) What is a soul? Explain the meaning of '*souls*' as used in "*When great souls die*"?

____

____

____

In "*When great souls die*", '*souls*' refers to human beings (persons).

(ii) According to the poem what happens to our reality bound to them when great souls die?
Great souls die and
our reality, bound to
them, takes leave of us.

(iii) According to the poem what happens to our souls when great souls die?
Our souls,
dependent upon their
nurture,
now shrink, wizened.

(iv) According to the poem what happens to our minds when great souls die?
Our minds, formed
and informed by their
radiance, fall away.

(v) What is a 'Great Tree' a metaphor for?

'Great Tree' is a metaphor for a person who is truly great, i.e., a person who has brought about a massive cultural change by his life and death. The 'Great Tree' in our life could be our parent(s), mentor, influential figure, a person who has left an indelible mark (with his/her good actions) on us.

Question 4.

Great souls die and
our reality, bound to
them, takes leave of us.
Our souls,
dependent upon their
nurture,
now shrink, wizened.
Our minds, formed
and informed by their
radiance, fall away.
We are not so much maddened
as reduced to the unutterable ignorance of
dark, cold
caves.

(i) According to the poem what happens to the air around us when great souls die?

____

____

____

(ii) According to the poem what happens to our memory when great souls die?

(iii) Explain the meaning of *Great souls die and*
our reality, bound to
them, takes leave of us.

(iv) Explain the meaning of *Our souls,*
dependent upon their
nurture,
now shrink, wizened.

(v) Explain the meaning of *Our minds, formed*
and informed by their
radiance, fall away.

(vi) What is a cave?

A cave is a hollow in the earth, especially one opening more or less horizontally into a hill, mountain, etc.

(vii) Explain the meaning of *We are not so much maddened*
as reduced to the unutterable ignorance of
dark, cold
caves.

Question 5.

And when great souls die,
after a period peace blooms,
slowly and always
irregularly. Spaces fill
with a kind of
soothing electric vibration.
Our senses, restored, never
to be the same, whisper to us.
They existed. They existed.
We can be. Be and be
better. For they existed.

(i) Explain the meaning of *Spaces fill*
with a kind of
soothing electric vibration.

(ii) Explain the meaning of *Our senses, restored, never*
to be the same, whisper to us.

(iii) What is the central theme which Maya Angelou explores in her poem *When Great Trees Fall*?

(iv) Give two examples of natural imagery from Maya Angelou's *When Great Trees Fall*?

(v) According to the poem, what is the effect of the passing away of great souls on people?

____

____

____

Interesting facts

1. The title of the poem '*When Great Trees Fall*' appears in
first line of the first stanza of the poem,
first line of the second stanza of the poem.

2. The word "great" appears four times in the poem. The word "Great" appears once in the title of the poem and once in the poem.

3. The word "small" appears once in the poem.

4. A number of word which begin with '*s*' / '*S*' appear in the poem. A few examples are:

shudder, safety, small, silence, senses, souls, sterile, see, suddenly, sharpened, shrink, so, slowly, Spaces, soothing.

5. The word '*souls*' appears four times in the poem.

6. The word '*senses*' appears twice in the poem.

7. The word '*existed*' appears thrice in the fifth stanza of the poem.

8. The word '*be*' appears twice in the second-last line of the fifth stanza of the poem and the word '*Be*' appears once in the second-last line of the fifth stanza of the poem.

9. The word '*be*' appears thrice in the fifth stanza of the poem and the word '*Be*' appears once in the fifth stanza of the poem.

10. A number of words which begin with '*b*' / '*B*' appear in the fifth stanza of the poem. A few examples are:
blooms, be, Be, better.

Multiple choice questions

(i) When great trees fall, _______________ on distant hills shudder.
(a) rocks
(b) lions
(c) elephants
(d) tigers

(ii) When great trees fall, _______________ hunker down.
(a) rocks
(b) lions
(c) elephants
(d) panthers

(iii) When great trees fall, _______________ lumber after safety.
(a) rocks
(b) lions
(c) elephants
(d) jackals

(iv) When great souls die, the air around us becomes
(a) light, rare, sterile
(b) heavy, rare, sterile
(c) light, dense, sterile
(d) light, rare, pure

(v) Which of the following statements is correct?
(a) We are not so much maddened as reduced to the unutterable ignorance of dark, cold caves
(b) We are so much maddened and reduced to the unutterable ignorance of dark, cold caves

(c) We are not so much maddened as reduced to the utterable ignorance of dark, cold caves
(d) We are so much maddened as not reduced to the unutterable ignorance of dark, cold caves

(vi) When great souls die then after a period peace blooms
(a) slowly and always irregularly
(b) slowly and always regularly
(c) quickly and always irregularly
(d) quickly and always regularly

Cues

(i) – (a) (ii) – (b) (iii) – (c) (iv) – (a) (v) – (a)

(vi) – (a)

[Trees help in the restoration of denuded soils. Trees are the natural purifiers of the environment. They are home to birds. They provide shelter, food, medicines, timber and essential oils.

A committee of five experts (Nishikant Mukerji, Soham Pandya, Sunita Narain, Bikash Kumar Maji, Niranjita Mitra) was set up the Hon'ble Supreme Court for the valuation of trees. According to the report filed by the committee, a tree is worth ₹74,500 a year {which includes cost of oxygen (₹45,000), cost of biofertilisers (₹20,000), cost of micronutrients and compost}. According to the committee, a heritage tree with a lifespan of well over 100 years could be valued at more than ₹1 crore. (This report dates back to 2020 – 2021 time-period.)

dendrology: the branch of botany dealing with trees and shrubs.

dendrochronology: the science dealing with the study of the annual rings of trees in determining the dates and chronological order of past events.

Trees have large storage capacities. Trees have carbohydrates, nutrients and water.]

A Considerable Speck

– Robert Frost

The author of this workbook retrieved the poem *A Considerable Speck* from https://www.public-domain-poetry.com/robert-lee-frost/considerable-speck-1129 on 16 August 2024 at 2030 hours.

A speck that would have been beneath my sight
On any but a paper sheet so white
Set off across what I had written there.
And I had idly poised my pen in air
To stop it with a period of ink
When something strange about it made me think,
This was no dust speck by my breathing blown,
But unmistakably a living mite
With inclinations it could call its own.
It paused as with suspicion of my pen,
And then came racing wildly on again
To where my manuscript was not yet dry;
Then paused again and either drank or smelt--
With loathing, for again it turned to fly.
Plainly with an intelligence I dealt.
It seemed too tiny to have room for feet,
Yet must have had a set of them complete
To express how much it didn't want to die.
It ran with terror and with cunning crept.

Colour is one of the key factors of visual communication. Colour might cause visual sensations or evoke sensory responses.

Darrel Abel in his article *Robert Frost's Range-Finding* detailed that Frost uses a mite as epitomes or atomies of man, to simplify and embody qualities of sentience, life-impulse, instinct or intelligence, and conscious will.

It faltered: I could see it hesitate;
Then in the middle of the open sheet
Cower down in desperation to accept
Whatever I accorded it of fate.
I have none of the tenderer-than-thou
Collectivistic regimenting love
With which the modern world is being swept.
But this poor microscopic item now!
Since it was nothing I knew evil of
I let it lie there till I hope it slept.
I have a mind myself and recognize
Mind when I meet with it in any guise
No one can know how glad I am to find
On any sheet the least display of mind.

Allen Carson Cohen in his article *Robert Frost's Arthropods* detailed that 17 of Frost's 347 poems are focused on insects, mites, or spiders.

Note: There are a few differences between Robert Frosts' *A Considerable Speck* which is printed in some books and Robert Frost's *A Considerable Speck* which appears in the Original Proof {https://www.jamescumminsbookseller.com/pages/books/237379/robert-frost/a-considerable-speck (accessed on 17 August 2024 at 1744 hours)} which are detailed below:

Line 3	Set off across what I had written there,
Line 5	To stop it with a period of ink,
Line 6	When something strange about it made me think
Line 7	This was no dust speck by my breathing blown
Line 10	It paused as with suspicion of my pen
Line 12	To where my manuscript was not yet dry,
Line 14	With horror, for again it turned to fly.
Line 16	It seemed too tiny to have room for feet
Line 20	It faltered! I could see it hesitate-
Line 25	Political collectivistic love
Line 26	With which the modern world is being swept-
Line 31	Mind when I meet with it in any guise.

The students are advised to refer to the poem which appears in the text-book prescribed by CISCE.

Word		Meaning
Considerable	:	worthy of attention, important
Speck	:	a small spot differing in color or substance from that of the surface or material upon which it appears or lies
beneath	:	below
idly	:	with no particular purpose
poised	:	held
period	:	the point or character (.) used to mark the end of a declarative sentence, indicate an abbreviation, etc.
mite	:	any of numerous small or minute arachnids of the order *Acarina*, including species which are parasitic on animals and plants or which are free-living, feeding on decaying matter and stored foods.
inclination	:	a liking or preference
manuscript	:	a book, document, letter, etc., written by hand
loathing	:	intense aversion
faltered	:	moved unsteadily
Cower	:	to crouch in fear
fate	:	destiny
Collectivistic	:	the socialist principle of control by the state of all means of production or economic activity
regimenting	:	to manage or treat in a rigid, uniform manner
microscopic	:	so small as to be invisible or indistinct without the use of the microscope
mind	:	the element, part, substance, or process that reasons, thinks, feels, wills, perceives, judges, etc.
guise	:	general external appearance

Punctuation mark statistics

Number of commas: 05
Number of period symbols: 10
Number of semi-colons: 02
Number of colons: 01
Number of dashes: 02
Number of hyphens: 02
Number of exclamation-marks: 01

Robert Frost's *A Considerable Speck* is a treatise on visual stimulus, imagination, intelligence, morality, enlightenment, empathy, 'reverence for life', sustained attention and 'power of observation'.

The poet-narrator is writing at his desk and he notices a mite walking across the sheet of paper on which he is writing. The mite has inclinations of its own. The mite paused and then raced wildly to the place where the ink on the manuscript had not yet dried, where it paused again and either drank the ink or smelt the ink with a feeling of intense dislike, for again it turned to fly.

Although the mite seemed too tiny to have room for feet yet it ran with terror and with cunning crept in order to express how much it didn't want to die. The mite faltered and then in the middle of the open sheet cowered down in desperation to accept whatever the poet-narrator accorded it of fate.

Since the poet-narrator could not associate the mite with anything evil whatsoever, the poet-narrator decided to let the mite lie there till he hoped the mite slept.

Terms used for the mite:
speck (*A speck that would have been beneath my sight*)
intelligence (*Plainly with an intelligence I dealt*)
poor microscopic item (*But this poor microscopic item now!*)

Terms used for describing the mite's behavior:

Terms	
racing wildly on paused again either drank or smelt-- With loathing it turned to fly ran with terror with cunning crept It faltered Cower down in desperation accept Whatever I accorded it off fate	these terms can be related with intelligence

Robert Lee Frost (26 March, 1874 – 29 January, 1963)

Robert Frost was born to William Prescott Frost, Jr. and Isabelle Moodie Frost. Robert married Elinor Miriam White in 1895. Frost was born in San Francisco. In August 1912, Frost and his family sailed for England. In 1915, Frost came back with his family to the United States. Frost was the recipient of four Pulitzer Prizes for poetry (1924, 1931, 1937, 1943).

Major works:

A Boy's Will (1913)
North of Boston (1914)

Examine the role of spatial setting in Robert Frost's *A Considerable Speck.*

A speck that would have been beneath my sight
On any but a paper sheet so white
suggests that the speck caught the poet-narrator's attention because of the white background.

Explain the meaning of:

I have none of the tenderer-than-thou

Collectivistic regimenting love
With which the modern world is being swept.

The world experienced an economic downturn in the 1929-1939 (approximately) period, which is referred to as Great Depression. During the 1929-1939 time-frame the output declined and the problem of unemployment was also witnessed.

Franklin D. Roosevelt spoke of a "New Deal" pertaining to actions for providing immediate economic relief as well as reforms in agriculture, finance, housing, industry, labour and waterpower thereby increasing the scope of the activities of the federal government (government-regulated economy).

Frost advocated the philosophy of *the largest possible number of citizens who could take care of themselves* as opposed to collectivism and regulation.

Various projects and programs such as Civilian Conservation Corps (CCC), Works Progress Administration (WPA), Tennessee Valley Authority were a part of the "New Deal".

Read the following extracts from Robert Frost's poem, '*A Considerable Speck*' and answer the questions that follow:

Question 1.

A speck that would have been beneath my sight
On any but a paper sheet so white
Set off across what I had written there.
And I had idly poised my pen in air

(i) What is a speck?

___

___

___

(ii) What does '*speck*' in "*A speck that would have been beneath my sight*" refer to?

____

____

____

(iii) Why did the poet-narrator idly poise his pen in air?

And I had idly poised my pen in air
To stop it with a period of ink.

(iv) Provide an instance from the poem which illustrates the concept of "recognition of life".

____

____

____

(v) How does the poet-narrator describe the motions/movements of the speck?

____

____

____

(vi) Provide an instance from the poem which illustrates the concept of "recognition of mind".

Question 2.

To stop it with a period of ink
When something strange about it made me think,

(i) What does "*it*" in "*To stop it with a period of ink*" refer to?

(ii) What does the word "*period*" mean?

(iii) What does "*it*" in "*When something strange about it made me think*" refer to?

(iv) In the light of "*When something strange about it made me think*" what did the poet-narrator "*think*"?

(v) What message is conveyed by the poem from which the above stanza is extracted?

(vi) Write a brief note on the poet who composed the poem from which the above stanza is extracted?

Question 3.

This was no dust speck by my breathing blown,
But unmistakably a living mite
With inclinations it could call its own.

(i) Explain the meaning of "*This was no dust speck by my breathing blown*"?

(ii) Is there an oxymoron in Robert Frost's *A Considerable Speck*?

[oxymoron: a figure of speech by which a locution produces an effect by a seeming self-contradiction, as in *working vacation.*]

(iii) Illustrate with the help of an example the use of visual imagery in Robert Frost's *A Considerable Speck.*

(iv) Provide three examples which illustrate alliteration in Robert Frost's *A Considerable Speck.*

[alliteration: the commencement of two or more stressed syllables of a word group either with the same consonant sound or sound group, or with a vowel sound that may differ from syllable to syllable.]

(v) What is a mite?

(vi) Explain the meaning of "*With inclinations it could call its own.*"

Question 4.

Then paused again and either drank or smelt--
With loathing, for again it turned to fly.
Plainly with an intelligence I dealt.

(i) What *paused again and either drank or smelt*? When and why did it pause before pausing *again*?

(ii) What is being referred to in *either drank or smelt*?

(iii) Explain: *With loathing, for again it turned to fly.*

___

___

___

(iv) Which *intelligence* is the poet-narrator referring to?

___

___

___

(v) Why do you think the poet-narrator feels that he was dealing with *intelligence*?

___

___

___

(vi) What is the difference between intelligence, knowledge and wisdom?

Intelligence is the ability to think logically, conceptualize and to abstract from reality.

Wisdom is the ability to understand nature (including human nature). In human nature, we find contradictions, paradoxes and change.

Information can be obtained by integrating data.

Knowledge can be obtained by integrating information.

Wisdom can be obtained by integrating knowledge.

A number of tests such as Stanford-Binet, Wechsler Adult Intelligence Scale have been developed for measuring intelligence.

Knowledge can be of several types: generic knowledge, domain specific knowledge, concrete and abstract knowledge, formal and informal knowledge, declarative and proceduralized knowledge, conceptual and procedural knowledge, elaborated and compiled knowledge, tacit knowledge, unstructured knowledge, structured knowledge, strategic knowledge, situated knowledge and metaknowledge.

Question 5.

I have none of the tenderer-than-thou
Collectivistic regimenting love
With which the modern world is being swept.

(i) Describe the actions which the mite exhibits in Frost's *A Considerable Speck.*

____

____

____

(ii) Explain: *Collectivistic regimenting love.*

____

____

____

(iii) Explain: *With which the modern world is being swept.*

____

____

____

(iv) What reason does the poet-narrator offer for letting the mite lie on the sheet of paper till he hopes it slept?

(v) With which thought does the poem *A Considerable Speck* conclude?

Question 6.

I have a mind myself and recognize
Mind when I meet with it in any guise
No one can know how glad I am to find
On any sheet the least display of mind.

(i) Give the meanings of the following words in the context of the stanza:

mind, guise, sheet

(ii) Summarize the views of the poem's persona pertaining to the arthropod.

The poem's persona recognized that the speck was not merely a fleck of dust but instead a living mite with inclinations it could call its own. The poem's persona decided to spare the mite's life rather than drowning it with the ink from his pen or killing it using any other method.

(iii) Is the view of divine intervention in worldly affairs suggested in Frost's *A Considerable Speck*.

(iv) Provide examples from Frost's *A Considerable Speck* which bring out the fact that Frost was anthropomorphic (ascribing human form or attributes to a being or thing not human).

(v) Explain the meaning of *I have a mind myself and recognize*
Mind when I meet with it in any guise
No one can know how glad I am to find
On any sheet the least display of mind.

Interesting facts

1. The word '*speck*' / '*Speck*' appears in the title of the poem, in the first line of the poem and in the seventh line of the poem.

2. The word '*sheet*' appears in the second line of the poem, in the twenty-first line of the poem and in the thirty-third line of the poem.

3. The word '*pen*' appears in the fourth line of the poem and in the tenth line of the poem.

4. The word '*paused*' appears in the tenth line of the poem and in the thirteenth line of the poem.

5. A number of words which begin with '*b*' / '*B*' appear in the poem. A few examples are:

been, beneath, but, breathing, blown, But

6. A number of word which begin with '*c*' / '*C*' appear in the poem. A few examples are:

could, call, came, complete, cunning, crept, Cower, Collectivistic

7. A number of words which begin with '*m*' / '*M*' appear in the poem. A few examples are:

my, made, me, mite, manuscript, must, much, middle, modern, microscopic, mind, myself, Mind, meet

8. A number of words which begin with '*p*' / '*P*' appear in the poem. A few examples are:

paper, poised, pen, period, paused, Plainly, poor

9. A number of words which begin with '*s*' / '*S*' appear in the poem. A few examples are:

speck, sight, sheet, Set, stop, something, strange, suspicion, smelt, seemed, set, swept, Since, slept

10. A number of words which begin with '*t*' / '*T*' appear in the poem. A few examples are:

that, there, To, think, This, then, Then, turned, too, tiny, to, terror, tenderer-than-thou, this

11. The sixteenth line contains three consecutive words which begin with '*t*'.
It seemed too tiny to have room for feet,

12. The twenty-fourth line contains four words which begin with '*t*':
I have none of the tenderer-than-thou

13. The twenty-sixth line contains three words which begin with '*w*':
With which the modern world is being swept

14. The last word of a number of lines in the poem ends with '*e*'. A few examples are:
On any but a paper sheet so white
Set off across what I had written there.
But unmistakably a living mite
Yet must have had a set of them complete
To express how much it didn't want to die.
It faltered: I could see it hesitate;
Whatever I accorded it of fate.
Collectivistic regimenting love
I have a mind myself and recognize
Mind when I meet with it in any guise.

15. The last word of a number of lines in the poem ends with '*t*'. A few examples are:
A speck that would have been beneath my sight
Then paused again and either drank or smelt--
Plainly with an intelligence I dealt.
It seemed too tiny to have room for feet,
It ran with terror and with cunning crept.
Then in the middle of the open sheet
Cower down in desperation to accept
With which the modern world is being swept.
I let it lie there till I hope it slept.

16. The last four lines of the poem can be interpreted in several ways:

I have a mind myself and recognize
Mind when I meet with it in any guise
No one can know how glad I am to find
On any sheet the least display of mind.

`Interpretation #1:` The poet-narrator says that he is blessed with intelligence and he can recognize the intelligence in others whichever guise it (the intelligence) may take. The poet feels extremely glad when he finds a display of intelligence on any sheet. The display of intelligence can refer to something like the mite or even the writing/typing on paper.

`Interpretation #2:` *I have a mind myself*: in a way speaks of self-recognition.
and recognize Mind when I meet with it in any guise: in a way speaks of the poet-narrator possessing the virtue of understanding and recognizing minds.
No one can know how glad I am to find: others cannot understand the poet-narrator's mind.
No one can know how glad I am to find
On any sheet the least display of mind: no one can know how delighted I feel when I find anything which makes sense on paper.

`Interpretation #3:` The poem's persona did not kill the mite on the sheet of paper on which he was writing because the mite displayed evidence of mind. The poem's persona respects a mind, recognizes a mind and feels glad on finding the display of mind on any sheet.

Multiple choice questions

(i) The speck in Robert Frost's *A Considerable Speck* refers to
(a) a dust speck
(b) a dead mite
(c) a living mite
(d) a symbol made by ink

(ii) Collectivism implies

(a) a theory or political system based on the principle that all industries and services should be owned by or for all the people in that country

(b) an economic system in which private actors own and control property

(c) private-enterprise

(d) free-enterprise

(iii) According to the poem *A Considerable Speck*, the poet narrator

(a) could not decide what to do with the speck

(b) removed the speck using a thinner

(c) let it lie there till he hoped it slept

(d) removed the speck using a whitener

Cues

(i) – (c) (ii) – (a) (iii) – (c)

Food for thought

(i) Discuss the role of colour in seeking visual attention?

___

___

___

(ii) entomology: the branch of zoology dealing with insects.

The Power of Music

– Sukumar Ray

The Power of Music is a poem from Sukumar Ray's *Abol Tabol* published in 1923. The poem was translated from Bengali into English by Prof. Sukanta Chaudhury. Sukumar Ray was the eldest son of the six children of Upendrakishore Raychaudhuri. The famous journal *Sandesh* was the brainchild of U. Raychaudhuri. Sukumar formed the *Nonsense Club* in 1906.

Abol Tabol is actually multilayered serious philosophy presented in a humorous manner. The reader will be able to perceive sense in nonsense, normality in abnormality, and rationality in irrationality in Sukumar Ray's oeuvre.

Satyajit Ray (the highly acclaimed filmmaker) was the son of Sukumar Ray.

Word		**Meaning**
hum	:	to make a low, continuous, droning sound; to sing with closed lips, without articulating words
strains	:	a passage of music or songs as rendered or heard
strain	:	a section of a piece of music, more or less complete in itself
staked	:	that which is wagered in a game, race, or contest
dazed	:	bewildered
rout	:	disorderly flight
languish	:	become weak or feeble
booming	:	making a deep, prolonged, resonant sound
broadside	:	any strong or comprehensive attack
brute	:	a nonhuman creature; beast

resent	:	to feel or show displeasure or indignation
blare	:	to emit a loud raucous sound
whine	:	to utter a low, usually nasal, complaining cry or sound
confounded	:	nonplussed
frantic	:	frenzied
soared	:	to rise or ascend to a height
welkin	:	the sky
mansion	:	a very large, impressive, or stately residence
billy goat	:	a male goat
sagacious	:	having or showing acute mental discernment and keen practical sense
bellow	:	to emit a hollow, loud, animal cry
whirled	:	turned around

Sukumar Ray's poem *The Power of Music* is marked with the use of hyperbole (obvious and intentional exaggeration; an extravagant statement or figure of speech not intended to be taken literally).

What is a lake? (*The fishes dived below the lake . . .*)

A lake is a body of fresh or salt water of considerable size, surrounded by land.

A lake has distinct zones: limnetic (pelagic), littoral, profundal, benthic.

The littoral zone is the near shore area where sunlight penetrates all the way to the sediment. The limnetic zone is the open water area where light does not penetrate to the bottom. The benthic zone is the bottom of the lake which has fine layers of mud.

On the basis of temperature, the layers of a lake are: epilimnion, metalimnion, hypolimnion.

Lakes can be of many types. A few examples are: amictic, holomictic, dimictic, polymictic, meromictic, oligotrophic, mesotrophic (eutrophic lakes, hypereutrophic), dystrophic.

Punctuation mark statistics

Number of commas: 22
Number of period symbols: 08
Number of semi-colons: 03
Number of apostrophes: 11
Number of exclamation marks: 01
Number of dashes: 02
Number of hyphens: 03
Number of interrogation-marks: 01

Sukumar Ray (30 October, 1887 – 10 September, 1923)
Sukumar Ray penned his first poem when he was only eight years of age.

Major works:
Abol Tabol
Khai Khai

Read the following extracts from Sukumar Ray's poem, *The Power of Music* and answer the questions that follow:

Question 1.

When summer comes, we hear the hums
Bhisma Lochan Sharma.
You catch his strain on hill and plain from Delhi
down to Burma.

[Burma (Myanmar):
shares borders with Bangladesh, China, India, Laos and Thailand;
has a coastline of 1,930 kms.
Nay Pyi Taw is the capital of Myanmar.]

(i) What information does the poem convey pertaining to Bhisma Lochan Sharma's singing inclinations?
Bhisma Lochan Sharma sings as though he's staked his life. Bhisma sings as though he's hell-bent.

(ii) What effect does Bhisma's singing have on the people?
The people, dazed, retire amazed although they know Bhisma's singing is well-meant. The people are trampled in the panic rout or languish pale and sickly. The people plead, "My friend, we're near our end, oh stop your singing quickly!" People cry, "We're going to die, oh won't you stop your singing?"
But Bhisma soars beyond the reach of the people no matter how much the people plead and grumble.

(iii) What effect does Bhisma's singing have on bullock-carts and horses?
The bullock-carts are overturned and horses line the roadside.

(iv) How does Bhisma respond to the effect of his singing on the people and animals around him?
Bhisma Lochan, unconcerned, goes booming out his broadside.
Bhisma soars beyond the reach of the people, no matter how much the people plead and grumble.

(v) What effect does Bhisma's singing have on brutes?
The wretched brutes resent the blare the hour they hear it sounded. They whine and stare with feet in air or wonder quite confounded.

(vi) What effect does Bhisma's singing have on fishes?
The fishes dive below the lake in frantic search for silence.

(vii) What effect does Bhisma's singing have on trees?
The trees collapse and shake – the crash can be heard a mile away.

(viii) What effect does Bhisma's singing have on the feathered fly?
The feathered fly turn turtle while they're winging.

(ix) What effect does Bhisma's singing have on the welkin?
The welkin weeps on hearing Bhisma's screech.

(x) What effect does Bhisma's singing have on the mighty mansions?
The mighty mansions tumble.

Question 2.

He sings as though he's staked his life, he sings
as though he's hell-bent;
The people, dazed, retire amazed although they
know it's well-meant.

(i) Whom does "*He*" in "*He sings as though he's staked his life*" refer to? How far (according to the poem) does the voice of the person referred to in the stanza above carry (travel) when he sings?
"*He*" in "*He sings as though he's staked his life*" refers to Bhisma Lochan Sharma. Bhisma Lochan Sharma's strain carries on hill and plain from Delhi down to Burma.

(ii) Explain the meaning of "*He sings as though he's staked his life, he sings as though he's hell-bent*".

____

____

____

(iii) How do the people respond to Bhisma's singing?

____

____

____

(iv) Dissect the range of emotions which Bhisma Lochan Sharma's singing evokes?

____

____

____

(v) It appears that most of the creatures are at the receiving end when Bhisma sings. Is there any creature who is able to counter Bhisma's singing?

A billy goat is able to counter Bhisma's singing.

Question 3.

He downs his horns and charges straight, with
bellow answ'ring bellow.

(i) Whom does "*He*" in "*He downs his horns and charges straight*" refer to and whom does "*He*" charge straight at?
"*He*" in "*He downs his horns and charges straight*" refers to a billy goat.
The billy goat charged straight at Bhisma Lochan Sharma.

(ii) Explain the meaning of "*He downs his horns*".
The billy goat lowers his head. In the context of the poem, when the billy goat lowers his horns, it indicates that he is preparing for charging or preparing for running towards an object (Bhisma Lochan Sharma) and hitting it (him) with its horns.
horns: the bony, projecting, often curved and pointed, hollow, permanent, paired growths on the upper part of the head of certain ungulate mammals, as cattle, sheep, goats, antelopes, etc.

(iii) Explain the meaning of "*charges straight*".
"*charges straight*" implies attacks aggressively without stopping (without losing time).

(iv) Explain the meaning of "*with bellow answ'ring bellow*".
The billy goat emits a loud deep sound while charging at Bhisma. Bhisma's singing is also characterized by loud deep sounds. The intensity of the billy goat's bellowing matches with the intensity of Bhisma's singing.

(v) According to the poem, what happens after "*He downs his horns and charges straight, with bellow answ'ring bellow*"?
The strains of song are tossed and whirled by blast of brutal violence, and silence prevails thereafter.

(vi) What is the message conveyed by the poem from which the above stanza is extracted?

Some of our habits or actions (or sometimes our behavior) might spell annoyance to others, although we may not want to annoy anyone (others) deliberately. The poem conveys the message that introspection and understanding the feedback which we receive might help in bringing a positive change in ourselves and in the people around us.

The poem also delivers a powerful message that just as Bhisma was hit by a billy goat, some known/unknown force of nature might hit us if we disturb others unnecessarily.

Question 4.

The strains of song are tossed and whirled by
blast of brutal violence,

(i) Explain the meaning of '*strains of song*'.

____

____

____

(ii) Explain the meaning of '*tossed and whirled*'.

____

____

____

(iii) What does '*blast of brutal violence*' refer to?

___

___

___

(iv) What is the effect of '*strains of song*' on some of the life-forms and non-life-forms as described in the poem from which the above stanza is extracted?

___

___

___

(v) According to the poem what happens after '*The strains of song are tossed and whirled by blast of brutal violence*'?

___

___

___

Interesting facts

1. A number of word which end with '*ed*' appear in the poem. A few examples are:
staked, dazed, amazed, trampled, overturned, unconcerned, wretched, sounded, confounded, dived, feathered, soared, tossed, whirled.

2. The name *Bhisma* appears in the second line, fifteenth line, twenty-ninth line and thirty-ninth line of the poem.

3.

The last word of the second line of the poem is '*Sharma*'.
The last word of the fourth line of the poem is '*Burma*'.

The last term in the sixth line of the poem is '*hell-bent*'.
The last term of the eighth line of the poem is '*well-meant*'.

The last word of the tenth line of the poem is '*sickly*'.
The last word of the twelfth line of the poem is '*quickly!*'

The last word of the fourteenth line of the poem is '*roadside*'.
The last word of the sixteenth line of the poem is '*broadside*'.

The last word of the eighteenth line of the poem is '*sounded*'.
The last word of the twentieth line of the poem is '*confounded*'.

The last word of the twenty-second line of the poem is '*silence*'.
The last word of the twenty-fourth line of the poem is '*hence*'.

The last word of the twenty-sixth line of the poem is '*winging*'.
The last word of the twenty-eighth line of the poem is '*singing?*'.

The last word of the thirtieth line of the poem is '*grumble*'.
The last word of the thirty-second line of the poem is '*tumble*'.

The last word of the thirty-fourth line of the poem is '*fellow*'.
The last word of the thirty-sixth line of the poem is '*bellow*'.

The last word of the thirty-eighth line of the poem is '*violence*'.
The last word of the fortieth line of the poem is '*silence*'.

Multiple choice questions

(i) According to the poem, when ___________ comes, we hear the hums.
(a) summer
(b) autumn
(c) winter
(d) spring

(ii) According to the poem you catch Bhisma's strain on hill and plain from __________ down to __________.

(a) Delhi, Chandigarh

(b) Delhi, Burma

(c) Delhi, Bhutan

(d) Delhi, Laos

(iii) According to the poem the fishes dived below the __________ in frantic search for __________.

(a) river, silence

(b) river, food

(c) lake, silence

(c) mountain in the lake, silence

(iv) According to the poem, __________ is a most sagacious fellow.

(a) Bhisma Lochan Sharma

(b) Bhisma Lochan Singh

(c) one of the men who hear Bhisma Lochan singing

(d) a billy goat

(v) __________ charged at Bhisma Lochan Sharma.

(a) A female goat

(b) A male goat

(c) An ox

(d) An elephant

Cues

(i) – (a)   (ii) – (b)   (iii) – (c)   (iv) – (d)   (v) – (b)

What is the Difference between a Hyphen and a Dash?

hyphen

A **hyphen** is used for combining words or for creating compound words, e.g., far-fetched.
(A hyphen is shorter than a dash.)

dash

A **dash** can be an em-dash or an en-dash.

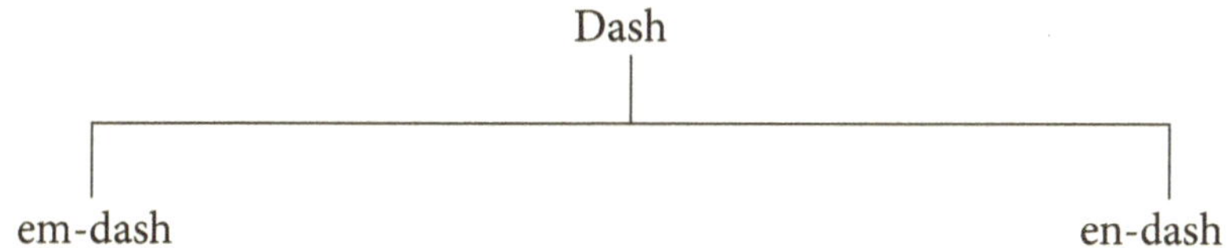

The **em-dash** is approximately the length of the letter M.
The **en-dash** is approximately the length of the letter N.

The em-dash is used for marking the explanatory element in a sentence.
For example: I will be proceeding at 07:00 a.m. — it is not dark at 07:00 a.m. on this part of the planet.
The en-dash is used for indicating a range, e.g., 17–23.

3-em dash is also used.

Quick Revision

Poem	*Haunted Houses*	*The Glove and the Lions*	*When Great Trees Fall*	*A Considerable Speck*	*The Power of Music*
Poet	H. W. Longfellow	Leigh Hunt	Maya Angelou	Robert Frost	Sukumar Ray
Number of stanzas	10	04	05	02 / 01	01
Number of lines in a stanza	04	06	The first stanza is of 06 lines. The second stanza is of 05 lines. The third stanza is of 13 lines. The fourth stanza is of 14 lines. The fifth stanza is of 11 lines.	The first stanza is of 29 lines. The second stanza is of 04 lines. (In some books, the poem is in a single stanza.)	40
Number of lines (The title of the poem is not included)	40	24	49	33	40
Original					'Ganer Gunto' (Bengali)

A Few Scholars of the English Language (Known for Their Timeless Work)

- Venerable Bede (*Historia ecclesiastica gentis Anglorum*) widely acknowledged as the 'Father of English History'
- Caedmon widely acknowledged as the first English poet
- Geoffrey Chaucer (*The Canterbury Tales*)
- Francis Bacon (*Commentarius Solutus*)
- Lindley Murray (*English Grammar*)
- John Milton (*Paradise Lost, Paradise Regained, Samson Agonistes*)
- Christopher Marlowe (*Tamburlaine the Great*)
- Ben Jonson
- William Shakespeare
- Edmund Spenser (*The Faerie Queene*)
- George Bernard Shaw (winner of the Nobel Prize for Literature in 1925)
- G B Shaw wrote *Pygmalion.* He won the Academy Award for his screenplay.
- T. S. Eliot (winner of Nobel Prize for Literature in 1948)

Wallace's note: There have been several literary giants (such as *Homer* and *Virgil*) who have contributed to different languages. It is not possible for me to list the names of all the literary artists.

The Nobel Prize in Literature

120 persons have been awarded the Nobel Prize in Literature in the 1901 to 2023 time-frame. The names of the Nobel Laureates in the 2014-2023 period are detailed below:

The Nobel Prize in Literature 2023	Jon Fosse
The Nobel Prize in Literature 2022	Annie Ernaux
The Nobel Prize in Literature 2021	Abdulrazak Gurnah
The Nobel Prize in Literature 2020	Louise Glück
The Nobel Prize in Literature 2019	Peter Handke
The Nobel Prize in Literature 2018	Olga Tokarczuk
The Nobel Prize in Literature 2017	Kazuo Ishiguro
The Nobel Prize in Literature 2016	Bob Dylan
The Nobel Prize in Literature 2015	Svetlana Alexievich
The Nobel Prize in Literature 2014	Patrick Modiano

Question. If $y! = y^3 - y$, then compute the value of y.

$y\,(y - 1)! = y(y^2 - 1)$

$(y - 1)! = (y^2 - 1)$

$(y - 1)\,(y - 2)! = (y^2 - 1^2)$

$(y - 1)\,(y - 2)! = (y - 1)\,(y + 1)$

$(y - 2)! = y + 1$

$(y - 2)\,(y - 3)! = y - 2 + 3$

$(y - 2)\,(y - 3)! = (y - 2) + 3$

$(y - 2)\,(y - 3)! - (y - 2) = 3$

$(y - 2)\,\{\,(y - 3)! - 1\} = 1.3$ or $(y - 2)\,\{\,(y - 3)! - 1\} = 3.1$

$\Rightarrow y - 2 = 1$ or $y - 2 = 3$

Thus, $y = 3$ or $y = 5$.

$y = 3$, does not satisfy the equation $y! = y^3 - y$.

If $y = 5$,

$5! = 5^3 - 5$.

Question. If $x^{14} = 49^x$, then find x?

$49^7 = 678223072849$

$7^{14} = 678223072849$

Question. If $3^x - 2^x = 65$, then find the value of x?

$(3^x)^{2/2} - (2^x)^{2/2} = 65.1$

$(3^{x/2})^2 - (2^{x/2})^2 = 65.1$

Let $a = 3^{x/2}$, and $b = 2^{x/2}$

$\Rightarrow a^2 - b^2 = 65.1$

$(a^2 - b^2) = (a + b)(a - b)$

$(a + b)(a - b) = 65.1$

$\Rightarrow a + b = 65, a - b = 1$

Therefore, $a = 33$, $b = 32$ (difficult to solve)

$(a + b)(a - b) = 13.5$ [13.5 = 65]

$\Rightarrow a + b = 13, a - b = 5$

Therefore, $a = 9$ and $b = 4$

$3^{x/2} = 9, 2^{x/2} = 4$

$3^{x/2} = 3^2, 2^{x/2} = 2^2$

Therefore, $x/2 = 2$

$x = 4$.

A Guide to Questions

Several experts who frame question papers make use of Bloom's Taxonomy.

Bloom's Taxonomy

A research paper pertaining to Learning Outcomes (Bloom's Taxonomy, summarized in Table 1 below) was published in 1956. It was revised by Krathwohl in 2002. The taxonomy is aimed at defining learning and assessment in an observable and measuring way.

Table 1. Bloom's Taxonomy

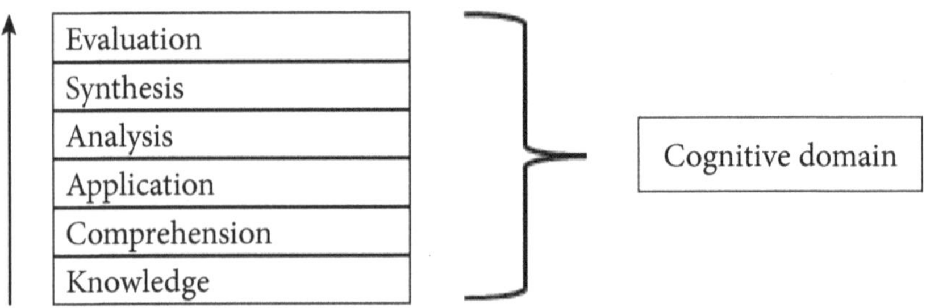

Table 2 will help in gaining a deeper understanding of the terms used in Table 1.

Table 2.

Knowledge	Knowledge of specifics	Knowledge of terminology
		Knowledge of specific facts
	Knowledge of ways and means of dealing with specifics	Knowledge of conventions
		Knowledge of trends and sequences
		Knowledge of classifications and categories
		Knowledge of criteria
		Knowledge of methodology
	Knowledge of universals and abstractions in a field	Knowledge of principles and generalizations
		Knowledge of theories and structures
Comprehension	Translation	
	Interpretation	
	Extrapolation	
Application		
Analysis	Analysis of elements	
	Analysis of relationships	
	Analysis of organizational principles	
Synthesis	Production of a unique communication	
	Production of a plan, or proposed set of operations	
	Derivation of a set of abstract relations	
Evaluation	Evaluation in terms of internal evidence	
	Judgments in terms of external criteria	

Table 3 lists a few Action Verbs which can be used for assessment of Learning.

Table 3.

Knowledge	List, define, recall, state, label, repeat, name
Comprehension	Translate, paraphrase, discuss, report, locate, generalize, explain, classify, summarize
Application	Operate, apply, use, demonstrate, solve, produce, prepare, choose
Analysis	Analyze, question, differentiate, experiment, examine, test, categorize, distinguish, calculate, contrast, outline, infer, discriminate, compare
Synthesis	Create, compose, argue, design, plan, support, revise, formulate
Evaluation	Rate, evaluate, assess, judge, justify

Source: A Pragmatic Master List of Action Verbs for Bloom's Taxonomy (Philip M. Newton, Ana Da Silva, Lee George Peters).

Questions with the Action Verbs detailed in Table 3 can be used for assessment of Knowledge, Comprehension, Application, Analysis, Synthesis and Evaluation faculties of the students.

Drama

(Julius Caesar by William Shakespeare)

Question

Read the extract given below and answer the questions that follow:

Brutus. [*Aside*] That every like is not the same, O Caesar,
The heart of Brutus yearns to think upon!

(i) Where is Brutus? Name any three other characters who are present along with Brutus? Account for their presence.

[The scene opens in a room in Caesar's house and Caesar enters in his nightgown.]

Brutus is in a room in Caesar's house.

Calpurnia, Decius, Publius, Ligarius, Metellus, Casca, Trebonius, Cinna, and Antony are present along with Brutus.

Calpurnia does not want Caesar to stir out of his house on the ides of March. She is there to dissuade Caesar from leaving the house.

Brutus, Casca, Trebonius, Ligarius, Metellus, Cinna have reached Caesar's house in order to take him (Julius Caesar) to the Capitol.

In Act II, Scene I, Cassius had said, "*But it is doubtful yet,*
Whether Caesar will come forth to-day or no;
For he is superstitious grown of late;
Quite from the main opinion he held once
Of fantasy, of dreams and ceremonies:
It may be, these apparent prodigies,
The unaccustom'd terror of this night,

Cassius expressed his apprehension that Caesar may keep away from the Senate-House on the ides of March.

And the persuasion of his augurers,
May hold him from the Capitol to-day."

Decius convinced the schemers that he would bring Caesar to the Capitol.
"*Never fear that: if he be so resolv'd,*
I can o'ersway him; for he loves to hear
That unicorns may be betray'd with trees,
And bears with glasses, elephants with holes,
Lions with toils, and men with flatterers:
But when I tell him he hates flatterers,
He says he does,—being then most flattered.
Let me work;
For I can give his humour the true bent,
And I will bring him to the Capitol."

Cassius then said, "*Nay, we will all of us be there to fetch him.*"

(ii) Why does Brutus say "*That every like is not the same*"?
Caesar invited the guests at his home to taste some wine along with him and used the term "*like friends*".
"*Good friends, go in, and taste some wine with me;*
*And we, **like friends**, will straightaway go together.*"
Brutus knows that some of the guests at Caesar's house (including himself) have hatched a plan of assassinating Caesar. [They are like arsonists in the guise of fire-fighters.] He, therefore says, "*That every like is not the same*".

(iii) Explain briefly what happens in the scene which follows the scene from which the above passage is extracted.

(iv) Mention any two aspects of Brutus's character which are revealed in the scene from which the above passage is extracted.

(v) What is the approximate time when Brutus says "*That every like . . . think upon!*"?
Eight o' clock in the morning.
[In Act II, Scene I, Brutus had said, "*By the eighth hour: is that the uttermost?*" Earlier in the scene from which the above passage is extracted, Caesar asked, "*What is't o'clock?*"
and Brutus replied, "*Caesar, 'tis strucken eight.*"]

(vi) Explain the significance of "*The heart of Brutus yearns to think upon!*"

(vii) Provide instances from the scene from which the above passage is extracted which illustrate the significance of the number three.

(viii) List any two similarities between Brutus and Caesar.

(ix) Give an instance of an Aside (other than the one in the passage above) from the scene from which the above passage is extracted.

(x) Some of the conspirators reach Caesar's house in Act II, Scene II. Is there any conspirator who does not reach Caesar's house in Act II Scene II?

The word "*come*" appears six times in the first fifteen lines of the confabulation between Decius and Julius Caesar in Act II, Scene II.

The word "*holiday*" appears thrice in Act I, Scene I:

Flav. Hence! home, you idle creatures, get you home:
Is this a **holiday**?...

Second Citizen. Truly, sir, to wear out their shoes, to get
myself into more work. But, indeed sir, we make **holiday**, to see Caesar, and...

Marullus...
And do you now put on your best attire?
And do you now cull out a **holiday**?...

INTERESTING POINTS

1. Raymond Queneau wrote a book *Cent mille millards de poèms* in 1961.

The book is 10 pages long, with 1 sonnet per page.

Each line of every sonnet can be replaced by a line at the same position on a different page.

Regardless of which lines are used, the poem makes sense.

(*Cent mille millards de poèms* is a book or a machine?)

2. Touchstone method

touchstone: a black siliceous stone used to test the purity of gold and silver by the colour of the streak produced on it by rubbing it with either metal.

touchstone: a test or criterion for the qualities of a thing.

There have been great poets like *Homer, William Shakespeare, Robert Frost, ...* The great works of poetry can act as touchstones.

3. A paper *'A Touchstone for the Bard'* authored by W. E. Y. Elliott & R. J. Valenza can be very useful for understanding mathematical analyses of text.

www.ingramcontent.com/pod-product-compliance
Lightning Source LLC
LaVergne TN
LVHW041110150826
845673LV00007B/2002